The Practical Youth Ministry Handbook

A START-TO-FINISH GUIDE TO SUCCESSFUL YOUTH MINISTRY

Compiled by Michael Warden

Group

D0018431

The Practical Youth Ministry Handbook
Copyright © 1993 Group Publishing, Inc.

Second Printing, 1994

Credits
Edited by Michael Warden
Designed by Dori Walker
Cover designed by Gary Templin

Contributors: Barbara Beach, Rich Bimler, Eric Bjork, Rick Chromey, Karen Dockrey, Donna Douglass, Lane Eskew, Dean Feldmeyer, Lonnie Fields, Mike Gillespie, Mark Gilroy, David Harris, Clinton Ibele, Gregg Johnson, Jan Johnson, Tom Klaus, Walt Marcum, Kevin McBride, Kevin Miller, Walt Mueller, Scott Noon, Arlo Reichter, Jolene L. Roehlkepartain, Joani Schultz, Thom Schultz, Margaret Smith, Yvonne Steindal, Michael Warden, Christine Yount, John Zehring

Scriptures quoted from the Youth Bible, New Century Version, copyright © 1991 by Word Publishing, Dallas, Texas 75039. Used by permission.

Library of Congress Cataloging-in-Publication Data
The Practical youth ministry handbook : a start-to-finish guide to successful
    youth ministry / compiled by Michael Warden.
        p.   cm.
    ISBN 1-55945-175-0
    1. Church work with teenagers. I. Warden, Michael D.
BV4447.P66   1993
259'.23—dc20   92-43278
                                                                CIP

Printed in the United States of America

Contents

PART 1: NO-FAIL FOUNDATIONS FOR YOUTH MINISTRY

PART 2: NO-FAIL IDEAS FOR YOUTH MINISTRY

Why Youth Ministry?

F ifteen or 20 years ago many church people viewed youth ministry as a babysitting service for teenagers. And often it was. Many youth ministries majored in roller-skating parties, hayrides, and goofy games.

Today fun and playfulness are still ingredients, but they're not the purpose of most youth ministries. Today's hyperbusy teenagers aren't looking to the church as a time-filler or yet another source of mere entertainment. Parents and church leaders know very well the heightened pressures and temptations facing kids in these complex times. They now see well-crafted youth ministries as necessary tools—preventive medicine—in a world of confusing and negative influences.

Today the church is coming to accept youth ministry as a real profession—and a ministry vital to the overall health of Christ's body. Christians have come to realize that there can be no greater priority than training their children in God's ways. And that's what youth ministry is all about.

WHAT IS YOUTH MINISTRY?

Put simply, youth ministry is the act of encouraging Christian growth in young people. That encouragement can take many forms—working on a car with a young person one-on-one, leading a Bible study, taking kids on a mission trip to Mexico, or throwing a block party for students from the local high school after a football game. All of these encourage Christian growth in

Why Kids Need Youth Ministry

Teenagers need a youth ministry that goes beyond Sunday school.

Why? The sad fact is that most teenagers who go to church aren't growing spiritually. A study by Search Institute revealed that:

- Two out of three teenagers say they've talked about their faith only once or not at all during the past year.
- Three out of four admit they haven't prayed daily in the past month.
- Three out of five say they haven't volunteered any time to help "the poor, the hungry, or the sick" within the past 30 days.
- Two out of three 10th- to 12th-graders aren't involved in Christian education.
- Nine out of 10 don't have a mature faith, according to a complex set of measurements devised by Search Institute.

According to the report, *Effective Christian Education: A National Study of Protestant Congregations,* only two out of five 16- to 18-year-olds surveyed say church challenges their thinking. And one out of eight says church is boring.

their own way. All of them are a valuable part of any church's attempt to draw kids into a deeper relationship with God.

From the outside, youth ministry can sometimes look imposing. Bible studies, monthly outreach programs, retreats, "gathering" parties, after-church get-togethers, mission trips—trying to get all these "activities" working in concert can seem like a challenge befitting the most skilled administrator. But at its heart, youth ministry is simply touching lives with Jesus' love. The activities used in youth ministry are nothing more than tools to help get kids and God together. The Holy Spirit does the rest.

HOW WILL THIS BOOK HELP?

The Practical Youth Ministry Handbook is a start-to-finish guide to building a successful youth ministry in your church. The foundational chapters in Part 1 contain important information that has been gleaned from the collective experiences and expertise of successful youth workers who have gone before you. In these pages, you'll find vital direction for developing and maintaining your youth ministry. And you'll get valuable tips on avoiding common mistakes others have made.

In addition, Part 2 of the book is full of ideas to get your ministry launched with a bang! All of these no-fail ideas have been tested time and again with teenagers from all over the world. They work, and they're yours to use as you see fit.

Follow the guidelines found in these pages, and you'll be standing on solid ground as you begin to reach out to kids with God's love. The greatest benefit of all will be the smiles you see from kids whose lives have been changed because of your efforts to touch them with God's love.

So dream big. Your involvement with the young people at your church can literally change the world.

Part 1:
No-Fail Foundations
for Youth Ministry

CHAPTER 1

Understanding Youth

"I have to tell you this—nobody in the youth group likes you."

What's this? A wide-eyed, serious-sounding seventh-grade girl from your group is telling you you're a flop? She's pulled you aside for a private talk after a church-camp activity in the mountains. She speaks with the self-assurance of an insider—an "old buddy."

Should you panic? Should you resign on the spot with a sobbing, penitent speech?

No.

Your seventh-grader is going through what adolescent development expert Jay Kesler calls the "Sherlock Holmes" stage. She's now intellectually adept enough to "correct" people. Strangely, because she loves and respects you, you're one of her first victims.

Tom Zanzig, editor of youth publications at St. Mary's Press, explains why this is typical of early junior high behavior. "Researchers tell us that junior highers have a preoccupation with their 'personal fable,' " he says, "This is the story they create about themselves. It's either, 'I'm wonderful. Nothing can hurt me,' or 'I'm nothing. Nobody cares about me.' So they think in extremes about themselves and others: 'Nobody likes me—or you, either, for that matter.' "

Because of this, don't be surprised if tomorrow that same seventh-grade girl pulls you aside and says, "Everybody likes you now." Her pendulum has swung to the other side.

So how do you respond to that seventh-grader's developing perspective? Put her in touch with reality. Ask questions that will help her think about her conclusions such as "What has someone said or done to make you think this?"

Kids' developmental phases explain how they interact, grow, and learn. Understanding their growing pains can restore your perspective when you're certain it's time to switch over to senior-citizen ministry. It can also give you ideas for programs and group goals.

Jane Vogel, who has worked with kids for years, and has also worked as an editor of SonPower Books, remembers a time when she tuned out kids' developmental needs. Just after she became a full-time youth director, church leaders warned her that the young adult group needed lots of guidance.

When the group decided to host a dinner for senior citizens, Vogel made sure every detail was perfect. The senior citizens were delighted. But the young adults were not. At the next meeting, they got down to business—"Jane, we think you should step down."

"As young adults, they wanted to take charge of their own projects," says Vogel. "They wanted me to be a resource person. So we worked out our own pattern. They asked questions such as 'We'd like to do something about social justice. What would be a good idea?' I gave them suggestions, and they chose the one they liked."

The chart on pages 14 and 15 outlines developmental characteristics for junior and senior high age groups. Some of the characteristics overlap among categories and age groups. There's a "+" behind those that also apply to the next older age group.

Why Do They Do That?

Before you look over the chart, see if you can answer the following quiz questions. The correct answers from the chart are referenced in parentheses after each question.

Junior Highers (seventh- to ninth-graders)

- Why do junior highers ask questions about sex no matter what the topic is? (2)

- Why is togetherness important even if they aren't having a deep discussion? (3)

- Why should you give junior highers a choice of several activities rather than asking, "What do you want to do?" (1)

Senior Highers (10th- to 12th-graders)

- Why is it good to let senior highers have specific input into their activities? (4, 5, 8)

- Why would a senior higher invest in a punk-rock wardrobe, and then abandon it after just two weeks? (6, 7)

- Why is it wise to withhold negative comments about senior highers' weird friends? (9)

Growing Pains

Junior Highers (seventh- to ninth-graders)

INTELLECTUAL	EMOTIONAL	PHYSICAL
They enjoy non-verbal creative expression. Their verbal skills aren't fully developed. They need structure and limits. They can't handle too many choices. (1) They have an odd sense of humor. They like to explore what's funny.	They have mood swings. They need successful experiences and achievements. They hibernate in self-preoccupation.	They experience rapid, uneven growth. They're self-conscious about appearance and have ravenous appetites. They enjoy vigorous activity but sometimes feel lethargic. They express confusion over sexuality with false bragging and conversations about sex. + (2)

Senior Highers (10th- to 12th-graders)

INTELLECTUAL	EMOTIONAL	PHYSICAL
They can organize, evaluate, and make choices. (4) They have verbal skills and talk well in small groups. They want to use their talents, creativity, and imagination. (5) They're curious. They want to know why. They enjoy odd-ball ideas. They look for recognition.	They're independent and don't always want to "do as they're told." They may be intense with emotional outbursts. They want acceptance so they adopt the hair styles, dress, and habits of friends. (6) They're forming personal identity and may try on new identities or values to see how they feel. (7)	They're curious about sex, especially pornography and masturbation. They experience rapid physical growth, ravenous hunger, and exhaustion.

SOCIAL	SPIRITUAL
They test authority but still want it. They need to belong to a group to help define who they are. (3)	They're ready for a more personal faith. They look for meaning in Bible stories and can identify with Bible characters.

SOCIAL	SPIRITUAL
They're more independent. They want more freedom. (8) They want to share themselves and develop friendships. They're loyal— even to "unusual" friends. (9) They need to practice Christian principles in a nonthreatening atmosphere.	They may branch out and serve on their own. They can apply skills learned in Bible study. They're defining their beliefs and convictions.

Free Developmental Resources

If you want to learn more about kids' developmental needs, check out these sources.

■ Search Institute, 122 W. Franklin St., Suite 525, Minneapolis, MN 55404. A research organization that collects data about children, adolescents, and families. Write for a free catalog and newsletter.

■ Center for Early Adolescence, University of North Carolina at Chapel Hill, Suite 211, Carr Mill Mall, Carrboro, NC 27510. A provider of information and training for professionals and parents who work with 10- to 15-year-olds. Write for a free newsletter.

EXPOSING THE NEEDS

Learning more about adolescent development goes a long way toward helping youth leaders understand their kids' general needs. But your kids aren't just figures on a chart. They're individuals, each with specific histories and personalities that translate into specific needs. How do you discover what the needs of your group really are?

The best approach is to conduct a needs analysis among your church's young people. Pages 17, 18, and 19 contain sample needs and interests inventories for your kids to complete. You may adapt or combine them to fit your young people. Be careful not to make any one survey look too long or too difficult to fill out. Remember to maintain confidentiality concerning the survey responses.

Strive to get full participation in your needs and interests analyses. One group even chose to "bribe" kids to complete the survey. After church services one Sunday, the planning task force

Youth Needs and Interests Survey 1

We're making plans for upcoming youth group programs. We want these programs to address your needs. But before we can address them, we need to know what they are. Help us by completing the following survey.

1. What are the top five worries or concerns in your life? (Check five only.)

_____ My relationship with God	_____ Money
_____ Making and keeping friends	_____ My parents might die
	_____ Loneliness
_____ Peer pressure	_____ Stress
_____ Drugs	_____ Cliques
_____ Drinking	_____ Divorce
_____ Doing well in school	_____ Self-esteem
_____ Dealing with temptation	_____ Prayer
_____ My looks	_____ Getting along with parents
_____ The future	
_____ College	_____ Music
_____ Nuclear war	_____ Suicide
_____ World hunger	_____ Sharing my faith
_____ Dating	_____ Cults
_____ Racism	_____ Other: _____

2. The biggest issue or concern in my life right now is _____
_____
_____
_____

THANK YOU!

Youth Needs and Interests Survey 2

We're making plans for upcoming youth group programs. We want these programs to address your needs. But before we can address them, we need to know what they are. Help us by filling in the blanks to the following statements.

1. One thing that really upsets me is _____

_____.

2. One thing I wish I could change about myself is

_____

_____.

3. One thing I would change about my parents is

_____

_____.

4. My life would be better if _____

_____

_____.

5. If I could ask God one question, I'd ask _____

_____

_____.

THANK YOU!

Youth Needs and Interests Survey 3

We're making plans for upcoming youth group programs. Help us make these plans by telling us which topics interest you. Circle a number for each item.

	INTERESTS ME									NO INTEREST	
Getting along with parents	10	9	8	7	6	5	4	3	2	1	0
Alcoholic parents	10	9	8	7	6	5	4	3	2	1	0
Single-parent households	10	9	8	7	6	5	4	3	2	1	0
Stepparents	10	9	8	7	6	5	4	3	2	1	0
Making friends	10	9	8	7	6	5	4	3	2	1	0
Relating to non-Christian friends	10	9	8	7	6	5	4	3	2	1	0
What to do on a date	10	9	8	7	6	5	4	3	2	1	0
How to be attractive to the opposite sex	10	9	8	7	6	5	4	3	2	1	0
On a date, how far is too far?	10	9	8	7	6	5	4	3	2	1	0
How do I know God's will for my life?	10	9	8	7	6	5	4	3	2	1	0
Why does God let bad things happen?	10	9	8	7	6	5	4	3	2	1	0
Coping with stress at school	10	9	8	7	6	5	4	3	2	1	0
Cliques	10	9	8	7	6	5	4	3	2	1	0
How to love myself	10	9	8	7	6	5	4	3	2	1	0
Why doesn't God answer my prayers?	10	9	8	7	6	5	4	3	2	1	0
Is it wrong for Christians to drink?	10	9	8	7	6	5	4	3	2	1	0
Dealing with temptation	10	9	8	7	6	5	4	3	2	1	0
What can we do about world hunger?	10	9	8	7	6	5	4	3	2	1	0
Dealing with peer pressure	10	9	8	7	6	5	4	3	2	1	0
What will I do after high school?	10	9	8	7	6	5	4	3	2	1	0
What college should I attend?	10	9	8	7	6	5	4	3	2	1	0
What can I do about loneliness?	10	9	8	7	6	5	4	3	2	1	0
I'm scared of losing someone close to me.	10	9	8	7	6	5	4	3	2	1	0
I worry about money.	10	9	8	7	6	5	4	3	2	1	0

Other: _____

Other: _____

THANK YOU!

kids set up a table covered with plates of fresh brownies. They lured the high-school-age kids to the table with the brownies. Then they said, "Take the survey and win a brownie." The ploy worked. Except some kids wanted to take the survey over and over.

The results of your survey should supply you with plenty of ideas for constructing the future of your youth ministry. You'll be better equipped to set some goals, and you'll know some of the pressing issues that need to be addressed in your programming.

Of course, surveys aren't the only means to discovering kids' real needs. As you continue in youth ministry, you'll need other tools for learning about what's going on in kids' heads—and hearts. To learn more about kids' needs, use these five field-tested strategies youth ministers use.

1. Ask kids to brainstorm. At the start of the year, use one of your normal meeting times for an informal "youth group family meeting." Tell kids the purpose of the meeting is to brainstorm ideas for three areas in the youth program—education, activities, and service projects. Then have kids think of topics or themes they'd like to study, activities or on-site programs they'd like to experience, and service projects they'd like to try.

2. Have kids respond to open-ended statements. By using open-ended statements, you'll get the best, most honest evaluation of kids' needs. Give kids each a handout with statements such as "I get so angry when..." "I wish I could..." or "It scares me to think about..." Make sure kids know their answers will be anonymous. Then collect the papers and go through them looking for common themes and topics.

3. Talk to kids' parents. If you want to know all of kids' needs, talk with kids' parents too. Ask parents to pinpoint changes in their kids' behavior and tell you why they think that behavior has changed.

4. Discover what kids talk about. Meet with schoolteachers. Be on the lookout for issues that at least two kids are talking about such as drug abuse. You can assume the rest of the kids deal with that issue at some level too. Also, develop personal relationships with teachers at nearby schools and actively seek out their perspectives on the problems kids face.

5. Survey adult leaders too. Since youth ministers are always playing "catch-up" to what kids are dealing with, try a three-pronged approach to determining their needs. First, survey your kids at the start of the school year. Ask them about areas of their lives they'd like to grow in or problems they're facing. Then ask your veteran volunteers the same questions you asked the kids. Finally, compare what kids say they need to what your adult volunteers say kids need. Look for prevalent themes.

Advanced Surveys

If you're interested in a more-detailed survey approach to determining your youth group's needs, buy the book *Determining Needs in Your Youth Ministry* by Peter Benson and Dorothy Williams of Search Institute (Group Publishing). Use this comprehensive book's handouts to survey your kids about their needs and interests. One group reported that before the leaders surveyed their kids, they had no idea kids were struggling with shoplifting and other "petty" crimes. And they didn't know kids feared losing their parents as much as they did. Share the general (not individual) results of the survey with parents and ask them how they interpret kids' answers.

As you learn more about the needs of your group members, you may discover quite a diversity of backgrounds and personalities. Some kids may come from abusive family backgrounds, others have had great parental role models. Several kids will probably come from single-parent or blended families. Some kids will be great students, others won't have a high value for education. Some may have become Christians when they were very young. Others may have accepted Jesus just last week.

So, how do you pull all this information together to create a unified youth ministry that effectively meets the needs of your kids?

The fact is that some of the branches of your ministry won't reach all your kids—and that's okay. You can tailor different parts of your ministry to different subgroups within your youth group. For example, starting an AA group for teenagers on your campus won't cause most kids to come banging down the doors. But for the handful that struggle with alcohol or come from alcoholic families that kind of ministry meets them right where they are.

Even with all this diversity, however, you can still create a unified youth group, consisting of all kinds of kids who all care about each other and enjoy doing things together.

How? By recognizing that for all their differences, there are some common denominators that will always draw teenagers together. So, as you scope out the framework of your ministry, consider these no-fail "commonalities" among kids.

1. All kids are part of the human race. Your teenagers have something in common with every other person who's walked the planet Earth. The core issues facing humankind are the same in Moscow, Russia, and Moscow, Idaho.

2. All kids want to be liked and accepted by other teenagers. Kids long for friendships with others their age. They desire admiration from peers of the opposite sex. They need to feel a sense of belonging—that they have some status within their peer group. And most are willing to pay the price for this acceptance—conformity.

3. All kids respond to caring adults. Not only do kids need positive adult interaction, they desire it! Seventy-six percent of teenagers wish their parents spent more time with them. Teenagers will spend as much time as possible with "older" people who take them seriously.

4. All kids are linked by adolescence. All kids are concerned about questions such as "What is happening to my body?" "How do I relate to the opposite sex?" "What will I do in the future?" "Who am I, and who will I be?" "What does it mean to be a Christian?" "How do I get along with my parents?" "How do I learn to love myself?"

Knowing kids' specific needs helps you determine the shape of your youth ministry. Understanding the common ground all kids share will help you build community in your group, and create an environment where kids reach out and touch each other with God's love.

It isn't enough to just meet kids' needs, after all. As a youth leader, you want them to become leaders too. You want them to learn how to reach out to others with Christ's love—just as you have reached out to them. It may sound paradoxical, but in youth ministry, your main goal should always be to "work your way out of a job." You accomplish this by teaching kids to do what you do, and then letting them do it. We'll talk more about this approach to ministry in the next chapter.

CHAPTER 2

Planning a Youth-Based Youth Ministry

At first glance, some people assume youth ministry is a bunch of kids doing whatever they want. That's far from the truth. Real youth ministry needs an organizational structure that links activities to goals and people to responsibilities.

There are several different models used to organize a youth ministry. But of all of these, there is none more need-centered and Christ-centered than the model called youth-based youth ministry. In this model, young people themselves do most of the planning, preparing, and executing for youth ministry programs, activities, and service missions. Organizing your youth ministry around this model will take some work, but it will be worth it to have the payoff of Christian growth in kids' lives.

Youth-based youth ministry begins at an "executive" level with the administrative team. This small group of adults oversees the youth ministry to assure that overall ministry goals are being met. Under the administrative team are the temporary planning task force and the ongoing steering committee, both of which are primarily composed of youth. These youth-based bodies plan the direction of the youth group. The chart on page 25 illustrates the paths of accountability created by this organizational structure.

An administrative team may already exist at your church. You might be calling it the "youth board," "youth council," or "youth ministry committee." Whatever it's called, it usually consists of adults, elected or selected, who have an interest in youth ministry. This body often oversees and supports youth ministry personnel, whether they're paid staff or volunteers.

This team should not include teenagers. Why? The administrative team's responsibilities include personnel issues—"hiring and firing" of adult volunteers, and so on. Highly sensitive information about volunteers is often discussed. Though young people's input may be important on issues such as these, the kids shouldn't be asked to assume the burden of adjudicating such delicate matters. Besides, the kids' energies and creativity are best used at the planning and action levels, rather than on the administrative level.

Youth Ministry Organizational Structure

Administrative Team
(quality control, recruiters for volunteer adults, resource providers, trainers, link to the congregation)

Temporary Planning Task Force
(writers of the "constitution" for the new youth ministry)
and
Steering Committee
(ongoing planners of programming, policy-makers)

Youth Group
(decision-makers, doers)

The administrative team performs several vital functions to ensure the ongoing success of your ministry. But the team's work is primarily "behind the scenes." The young people may never know about much of the work of the administrative team. And that's okay.

Here's a look at the administrative team's duties.

1. Supervising. The administrative team serves as a guide and as a quality control for the planning task force, steering committee and youth group. This team assists the adult youth workers by keeping the goals and practices of the overall ministry in focus.

2. Recruiting adult volunteers. Not every adult works well with teenagers. Some adults who offer to help should be steered to other ministry opportunities. And others who've never offered their services should be pursued to work with kids. The administrative team screens, recruits, and assigns adults to help in youth ministry roles. Chapter 3 includes additional information about finding adult leaders.

3. Training. The administrative team is responsible for training the adults who work with kids and for the kids who lead other kids. If they have the necessary expertise, members of the administrative team may do the training themselves. If not, they'll need to call in other resource people to provide training.

4. Appointing key people. The administrative team should select an adult who will chair the steering committee, which handles the ongoing business of the youth group. This steering committee is made up of youth and adults and is in many ways the backbone of youth-based ministry. The adults who serve on this committee have the power to "make or break" youth-based ministry.

5. Evaluating. The administrative team observes the progress of the youth ministry and offers suggestions for improvement. These evaluation duties usually include assessments of adult volunteers. The administrative team determines whether specific volunteers should be invited to serve another term. The team also is charged with the unfortunate responsibility of "firing" a volunteer whose behavior has a negative influence on the kids.

6. Encouraging the planning task force and steering committee. Young people and adults working on various youth ministry tasks can become discouraged. Temporary setbacks can deflate enthusiasm. Here's where the administrative team can step in and remind everyone of the ministry's goals and the progress it has made.

THE PLANNING TASK FORCE'S ROLE

The planning task force, comprised of a few young people and adults, serves the vital function of building a constitution for the youth ministry, and then mobilizing people and resources to breathe the ministry to life.

More than half of the task force should be young people. A planning task force populated primarily by adults tends to stifle kids—even if the adults don't talk much.

Have the administrative team appoint the adults who serve on the task force. The teenagers who serve may be elected or selected by the administrative team. The choice is yours.

The first job of the task force is to determine the needs of kids in your youth group. By using various surveys, such as those found in Chapter 1, the task force should get a pretty good idea of kids' needs and the direction the youth ministry should go.

Once the needs are known, the task force now begins to frame the "constitution" of your church's youth ministry. Many questions need to be answered and many far-reaching decisions need to be made. Here's an overview of the issues your task force will need to address.

1. Establish a purpose. What is the end-goal of your youth ministry? Why should it exist? Ask for ideas and write all of them on a chalkboard. Once you've written everyone's ideas, ask each task force member to write a statement of purpose for the youth ministry. It may be a sentence or a short paragraph. From these suggestions, press for a consensus on one condensed statement that pleases the entire task force.

Your Youth Ministry IQ

It takes more than activities and counting numbers to involve young people. Group members need to feel important and necessary in youth ministry before they become involved.

To see how well you involve group members, take a few minutes to test your youth ministry IQ (involvement quotient).

Put a checkmark in the box beside each item you already are doing.

❏ Build in a few surprises through mystery trips, great desserts, surprise visitors, brain teasers, and other ideas.

❏ Spark interest with creative fliers.

❏ Encourage and allow spontaneous laughter.

❏ Use crazy skits and energetic games.

❏ Publicize events over and over.

❏ Make yourself available to group members.

❏ Vary meeting locations from time to time.

❏ Create an environment where kids feel loved and free to share concerns.

❏ Accept kids' responses as important all the time.

❏ Let young people take responsibility for their own learning.

❏ Use kids' names frequently during discussions.

❏ Thank kids for sharing their thoughts during a meeting.

❏ Rely on the power of the Holy Spirit.

❏ Challenge kids to make a personal commitment to Christ.

❏ Encourage a consistent, daily approach to Bible reading.

❏ Share your own faith-journey with kids.

❏ Encourage questions about God.

❏ Implement programs and retreats that focus on spiritual growth.

❏ Promote weekly attendance in church.

- ❏ Plan a balanced ministry.
- ❏ Accept that most young people can't attend everything.
- ❏ Involve kids in leadership.
- ❏ Ask group opinions on ideas and scheduling.
- ❏ Follow up with appreciation notes and calls when group members complete leadership tasks.
- ❏ Confront disruptive behavior through private one-on-one discussion.
- ❏ Address putdowns and ridicule when they occur.
- ❏ Understand that kids are busy.
- ❏ Don't take it personally when kids fail.
- ❏ Help group members weigh choices and accept whatever decisions they make.
- ❏ Make service and outreach an important part of the group.
- ❏ See each young person as a unique child of God.
- ❏ Discover at least one talent in every teenager and affirm it.
- ❏ Notice when someone is down and try to help.
- ❏ Take each group member out for a meal at least once during the year.
- ❏ Use the phone frequently to see how kids are doing.
- ❏ Have kids assist in church services.
- ❏ Have kids lead one entire worship service at least once a year.

Total the number of checkmarks. If you checked all 37 items you have an incredible foundation for involving young people. A score between 30 and 36 still rates you an A—GREAT JOB. A score between 24 and 29 deserves a good strong B. If you have fewer than 23 checkmarks, use this test for ideas on how to help involve group members more.

2. Determine a member profile. Is the group for junior high and senior high combined? combined all the time—or just on special occasions? What about high school graduates? When are kids old enough to join the group?

Do we design the group based on the interests of kids in our church, or the unchurched kids in our community? What will happen if we attract unchurched kids that aren't the type our regular members want "hanging" around?

3. Form a schedule. Should your group meet weekly? twice a week? What's the best day to get together? What time should the meeting begin? How long should it last? Where should you hold your meetings? What are the advantages to meeting in homes? in the church building?

4. Design formats for meetings and schedules. What are the essential elements that should be included in every meeting? What are the highest values we want kids to understand? Worship? Affirming relationships? Bible knowledge? Social involvement? How can our meeting formats reflect those values?

How many special events should we have each month? Who are the special events for—regular attenders or potential new youth? How many retreats or mission trips should we plan each year? What should be the purpose of these trips? What's the best way to plan for these trips?

5. Design a steering committee. After the temporary task force has finished its work, you'll need an ongoing team of youth and adults to plan programs and handle administrative decisions.

The task force should decide the shape of this steering committee. How many young people should serve on it? Should each age group be represented? How and when will they be elected? How long will they serve?

6. Clarify the roles of adults. A strong team of adult volunteers is needed for any youth ministry to remain healthy and growing. The task force should determine exactly what role adult volunteers will fill and how long their terms of service should be. One task force developed a list of desired qualities and possible duties of adult volunteers. Use it to help your own task force create an appropriate "job description" for volunteers.

"We want our adult volunteers to
   help lead some activities,
● be 'temporary parents,'
● help supervise,
   support the group members,
● provide crowd control,
● listen to youth,
   help with decisions,
   trust youth,
   share their faith, and
   let kids lead."

7. Solidify your "constitution." Your task force will be working hard to build the foundation for your youth ministry. Unless steps are taken, much of this effort may dissolve in time. So, the task force may wish to build in some stability and longevity to its decisions. Perhaps your team will require that its foundational decisions need a two-thirds majority vote by the group to overrule. Also, be sure the decisions of the task force are typed and assembled into a constitution type of document. It's important to have a tangible record to refer to rather than someone's memory.

8. Plan the "launch." Once the basics are decided, the task force is ready to plot the first few months of the youth group's life. It's important to launch the ministry schedule with a special kickoff event. Also, the task force should organize and prepare the youth group meetings for the first three months or so. This will give the new steering committee a chance to get organized during that planned period.

THE STEERING COMMITTEE'S ROLE

Once your planning task force has completed its work and your youth ministry is launched, the steering committee takes over. This committee is, in many ways, the "nerve center" of a youth-based ministry. Though the administrative team supervises the entire youth ministry, it's the steering committee that actually forms the plans and creates much of the programming. Let's take a look at this team's crucial duties.

1. Setting priorities. This team struggles with tough questions such as "Are we successfully encouraging Christian growth in our group?" "Do we have a good balance of nurture and outreach?" "How are we ministering to the inactive kids in our group?" "Is our ministry attractive to unchurched young people?" "How much time should we devote to fun versus spiritual growth programs?" "Are we involving all the kids in our group?"

2. Planning. The steering committee tackles the tough job of planning future youth group meetings, programs, projects, retreats, and special events. Once plans are initiated, the steering committee often delegates responsibilities to other young people or task forces.

3. Setting policies. Like any organization, youth ministry needs rules, guidelines, and procedures to operate smoothly. The steering committee makes many policy decisions itself and refers others to the whole group whenever necessary.

4. Handling discipline problems. A few young people in any group will always challenge the authority and break the rules. Many of these cases are best handled by the rule-breakers' peers—the kids on the steering committee.

EVALUATION

One essential element in youth ministry is evaluation. Without looking at the positives and negatives of your ministry, you'll never know what you're doing right—and what could use some improvement. Ongoing evaluations can be done in several ways.

1. By the adult volunteers. Ask for all your adult volunteers to meet for coffee or ice cream. Let them express their praise and concern for the youth ministry. Ask them to share ways to solve problems, decide which issues need to be brought before the steering committee, and so on.

2. By the steering committee. Using this group of evaluators keeps the ownership of fine-tuned quality ministry in the kids' hands. They see themselves as a vital ingredient in the success of the ministry. Ask the committee to share disappointments and wrestle with solving problems. Also, be sure to celebrate ministry successes.

3. By the whole group. Occasionally, it's helpful to ask the entire group for feedback. This can be accomplished by written surveys. Include open-ended statements such as "What I really like about our meetings is..." or "One thing I want the group to focus on more is..."

With creativity, hard work, and honest evaluation, your youth ministry can meet many needs and draw young people closer to Christ.

CHAPTER 3

Cultivating Leadership

T he #1 reason youth workers abandon their ministry is burnout. And youth workers say the #1 reason they burn out is "overwhelming job responsibilities." So what's the antidote to overwhelming job responsibilities?

State-of-the-art volunteer management, combined with the goal of developing kids as leaders.

This twofold approach to ministry can seem a bit tricky at first. You don't need adult volunteers who you can count on to support only you. You need adult volunteers you can count on to support kids—and their development as leaders. Volunteers need to be able to lead, but they also need to be able to step aside and let kids lead.

Most adults suffer from a chronic case of rescue-itis. We want to believe kids can do it, but there's a smidgen of mistrust. What if they forget the refreshments? What if Sandy doesn't show up to lead the game? Or worse yet, what if she leads it, and it really bombs?

Finding youth workers who can walk the line between leading and letting go can be challenging. But the effort you make now will pay off in the long run—both for you and your youth group.

As your administrative team begins the search for adult volunteers, follow these steps.

1. Search for candidates. Begin by brainstorming names of potential adult workers—people you know and those you know little about. Next, evaluate your list based on what you've observed about each person's gifts and ability to work with young people. Ask hard questions such as "How active are these people in church?" "In what situations have we seen them relating with teenagers?" "How willing are they to let kids lead? be flexible? allow kids to fail?" "How much time can they realistically give to the youth program?"

2. Brainstorm criteria for volunteers. Ask your team members to each list expectations and qualities they look for in adult leaders. Ask them to each answer the question, "What do volunteers do?"

Combine the answers to create a list of volunteer qualities you're looking for. One team produced a list of 26 qualities, including a sense of openness, a caring and concerned attitude, the ability to listen, a respect for young people, creativity, stability, personal warmth, a sense of humor, and patience.

That same group further distilled its list by deciding on three primary criteria for volunteers:

● a deepening commitment to Jesus Christ and his body,

● an ability to share their faith with others, and

● a desire to help lead group members into greater spiritual and personal growth.

3. Create a job description. Once you've brainstormed all the qualities and duties you want your volunteer youth workers to have, put all that information in a concise job description that defines what you're looking for—both in terms of qualities and responsibilities. See the "Sample Job Description" on page 36 for ideas on how to put your own job description together.

4. Develop an interviewing strategy. Before you set appointments with prospective volunteers, talk about questions you'd like to ask and answers to questions you'll likely be asked.

Sample Job Description

We believe it's important for adult volunteers to share their faith in Christ and their commitment to the church with the members of our group and to do so with caring and concern.

We expect all youth workers to live out the character of Christ in their lives—both personally and in ministry with youth. Specifically, we expect each youth worker to

■ guide the steering committee and the youth group in decision-making, and in planning and implementing those decisions;

■ be creative in offering new ideas for group activities;

■ be available and flexible in the amount of time given to the group—attend weekly meetings and at least half of our scheduled activities, and make a six-month, renewable commitment;

■ accept who we are, respect us, and relate to us as our adult friends;

■ work with the youth pastor, the administrative team, the steering committee, and the young people to achieve the goals set forth by the youth ministry constitution.

Choose self-revealing questions such as "What are your interests?" "What are your goals in working with teenagers?" "What are your expectations of the group?" "Most important, why are you interested in becoming a youth volunteer?"

5. Meet with volunteer candidates. In the interview, discuss the job description and go through your list of questions. Allow your candidates time to ask you questions. After the interview, take your administrative team out for coffee or lunch to talk over their feelings and impressions.

6. Present new volunteers to the church. After you've successfully recruited volunteers, have your administrative team call the youth group members to let them know. Then have one team member formally introduce your new volunteers to the congregation.

Forming a strong adult leadership team brings you to a starting point for the second phase of leadership development—raising up kids as leaders. Now let's look at the best way to accomplish the goal of "working your way out of a job."

Why People Volunteer

A study by Psychology Today reported that people have volunteered more in recent years than they did a decade ago. These are the top eight reasons people say they volunteer.
- I want to help others.
- I enjoy the work.
- The specific work or cause interests me.
- I feel a responsibility to volunteer.
- Someone I know asked me to volunteer.
- I have free time on my hands.
- I want to make new friends.
- I want to get job experience.

To let go and allow kids to take responsibility may be one of the best (and the hardest) gifts we give to our youth group members. Instead of knocking kids—wondering why they're not more responsible—we need to recognize that the responsibility begins with us. Yes, us.

Create kids you can count on by practicing these five steps.

1. Believe in young people. That's it. Simply believe in them. Your attitude will rub off, and pretty soon they'll believe in themselves!

2. Dole out doable chunks. Give young people responsibilities they can successfully manage. It's a rare teenager who can pull off planning an entire lock-in. But a normal teenager can help plan the lock-in's Bible study time.

The "responsibility rate" in kids rises in proportion to two elements:

● **The specific guidance you give.** For example, compare "Steve, you're in charge of planning a half-hour Bible study, complete with an activity to get us into the scripture, and follow-up discussion questions" to "Steve, you're in charge of the Bible study."

● **The task's perceived importance.** Compare "Trish, we'd like you to come early and help set up chairs in a circle. Getting ready early helps group members know we're prepared. And the circle of chairs puts us all at an equal level when we start" to "Trish, we need you to set up chairs."

When you convey specifics for the task and the task's value, you help kids feel they can do it.

3. Remember: Teenagers are teenagers. In an age when kids work part time, buy groceries, fix meals, and are expected to grow up fast, it's important not to heap guilt and inappropriate expectations on a 15-year-old. If you tell José that he's in charge of a fun fest next month, and you say nothing more until the day before the event, José probably will have forgotten. He's young. Don't expect him to be anything other than who he is.

4. Support kids. Before, during, and after the moments teenagers are doing their duties, encourage them. A wink, a nod, a surprise postcard, a squeeze on the arm, a "good job" spoken in front of the group, even a positive remark to a parent—all these show young people we believe in them and want them to succeed.

5. Allow for failure. We want teenagers to grow by tasting success—and celebrating it. But we know success isn't the only way to grow—in fact, it's not always the best way. Failure may be an even greater teacher. Failures can transform bombs into benefits, if we take time to debrief what's happened and help kids choose growth.

Allowing for failures is tough, but wise. Caring adults use failures as great teachable moments. Look at what God did. He turned a devastating Good Friday "failure" into a glorious Resurrection!

USING PARENTS AS VOLUNTEERS

The question frequently arises: What about using parents of group members as adult helpers? Generally, the best answer is: not in group leadership roles.

Young people should feel free to talk openly in the youth group. But with parents present—even wonderfully creative and loyal parents—kids inevitably feel stifled. Suppose a group discussion emerged on the subject of parents. Would any young person respond in the same way if his or her parent were present?

Also, adult volunteers themselves need to feel free to share candidly in group discussions. How many parents would talk openly about their inner struggles if their own kids were sitting across the room? In addition, how many adult volunteers would feel free to openly discuss a problem in the youth group that involved the child of a parent sitting next to them in the meeting?

And what happens if a parent adult volunteer doesn't work out? What if you're faced with asking a parent to withdraw from his or her position? How will that parent feel about the ministry?

How will the parent's reaction affect his or her child? How will the teenager's reaction affect the rest of the group?

This is not to say that using parents as youth volunteers never works. In truth, it often does. There are many significant roles parents can fill in your youth ministry. We'll look more at what those roles are in Chapter 4.

Involving Parents

"I feel like the lonely, unloved sheriff in an old black-and-white western," said Matt, tears forming in his eyes. "I came to First Church to minister to kids. I've done the best I can, but the parents are ready to run me out of town anyway."

Matt's listeners—a weekly fellowship of youth leaders—nodded their heads. They understood his emotions.

Sandy leaned forward, his jaw set. "I spend 70 hours a week loving and caring for these kids and I don't think their parents care!" he fumed. "Can't they see I'm trying to help them?"

Maybe not.

In most youth ministries, youth leaders deal with all kinds of parents—some who think the leaders are a godsend and some who wish God would send the leaders away. In your ministry, you may face the same confusing messages.

But much of the frustration with unsupportive parents can be avoided by your approach to ministry. Investing in a youth ministry that lacks parental support is risky. So rather than digging in to protect the vision for ministry God has given you, broaden your vision to include parents too.

How? Become a "parent supporter." Make the choice to stand behind parents as they assume their God-given responsibility to nurture their kids in the Christian faith. You'll be amazed at the support you'll receive from parents and the increased effectiveness of your ministry.

As you saw in the last chapter, using parents as volunteer youth workers usually isn't the best solution to gaining parental support. But these steps will help you work toward creating a team spirit between you and kids' parents.

1. Take your job seriously. Whether you're paid or a volunteer, view yourself as a professional who's also an adult. Act like an adult. Work hard, prepare well, and be a lifelong learner. Remember, respect is earned.

2. Let parents know you're trustworthy. What parents would allow their child to go on a two-week mission trip with someone they don't trust? Parents will support youth workers who've worked hard to gain their trust.

Start and end your meetings on time so parents aren't waiting in the parking lot. Don't leave promises unfulfilled. Take precautions to ensure the safety of kids. You'll earn their trust when you attend to the little concerns that often go unnoticed.

3. Support parents. Don't ever put down a parent in a conversation with a young person. Whenever possible and appropriate, affirm parents in front of their teenagers. Always speak highly of the role of a parent in kids' lives and recognize that parenting is a tough job even in the best of circumstances.

4. Keep family interests in mind. Families are bombarded with commitments from all sides. They're pulled in as many directions as there are family members. Give families a chance to be together. Avoid scheduling major trips and events on special holidays. Publicize your schedule at least four months in advance so parents know what's going on. Don't schedule meetings at meal times. And remember that families live on limited budgets. Don't bleed them dry with expensive youth activities.

5. Keep parents informed. Parents appreciate a youth worker who keeps them well-informed. Here's a good communication rule of thumb: Tell every parent everything in as many attractive ways as possible.

Get the word out through fliers, mailings, calendars, newsletters, church bulletins, bulletin boards, and telephone hot lines. And when you distribute information about youth events, be sure to include all the pertinent information parents need to know.

6. Listen. Parents probably know their kids better than anyone in the youth ministry structure. Listen to their advice. When youth parents ask to talk with you about the ministry, take the time to hear them out. Then ask them to write down their major concerns or comments, so you can more effectively think about what they're saying. Bring the parents' written comments before your administrative team or, if appropriate, your steering committee. Then tell the parents how their concern was dealt with and what decision was made. Asking parents to jot down their concerns serves several purposes.

● It allows you time to seriously consider what they're saying.

● It keeps a record of exactly what the parent is saying, so there is less chance for misunderstanding.

● It allows you to avoid being the "heavy," by sharing the decision-making process with the administrative team or the steering committee.

● It helps the parent know that their comments and concerns will be taken seriously.

In addition to this, hold parent meetings at least twice a year to give parents a voice in what they see as the strengths and weaknesses in the youth ministry.

7. Communicate your ministry philosophy. What are you trying to accomplish through your youth ministry? Inquiring parents want to know. Give parents a copy of your youth ministry constitution. Hand it out at your parents meetings and mail it to the parents of any new teenager who joins your group.

8. Be a parenting resource. In *The Five Cries of Parents,* Merton and Strommen identify the "cry for outside help." Parents can't go it alone. The pressures and needs of parenting are too great.

So offer classes on parenting skills. Plan seminars and special programs to address specific concerns such as drugs and drinking, the occult, or teenage sexuality. Start help groups for parents dealing with family violence. Help parents identify their needs and steer them toward the resources that can meet those needs.

By the way, being a resource to parents isn't dependent on whether or not the parents are Christian. Non-Christian parents share most of the same concerns as Christian parents. And your training sessions might just provide an opportunity to share your faith with non-Christian parents.

9. Build support networks. Give parents a chance to get together as parents and discuss parenting concerns. You can do this through specialized Bible studies or parenting support groups.

Reaching Non-Christian Parents

In even the most accepting ministry environment, reaching non-Christian parents can be challenging. Use these tips to help you bridge the gap between death and new life.

■ **Teach kids to admit to their parents when they're wrong.** Most parents would drop dead if they heard, "I was wrong," coming from one of their teenagers. Teach kids to walk in open repentance for the sins they commit at home.

■ **Encourage kids to be thankful.** Challenge young people to come up with creative ways to express thankfulness in the home. Have a brainstorming session. Then ask each person to try one "thankfulness" idea.

■ **Ask kids to be "overobedient."** This is a key factor in influencing non-Christian parents for Christ. Many young people today do just enough to get by. But God's way is to do more than is expected.

■ **Reach out to parents through the media.** Develop a "parents only" newsletter. Plan daylong seminars that address parents' needs. Develop a resource library on parent-teen relationships, and then advertise it to parents. These ideas can draw a non-Christian parent toward a relationship with Christ, because they communicate to the parent that he or she matters to God.

■ **Meet parents on their turf.** When you get the opportunity to visit a family at home, take it. Don't use the opportunity to "sell" your church to parents or even to promote your youth ministry. Use it just to build relationship with parents. Doing this communicates to them that you have no hidden motives and that you genuinely care about them.

■ **Meet parents on your turf.** Consider holding parents' meetings in your home. This may be less imposing for non-Christian parents than a church setting, and it also communicates your willingness to open your life to parents.

10. Encourage parents to be together. Serve families by scheduling several family-oriented activities for kids and parents to attend together. Make the activities as nonthreatening as possible, so as not to scare off families with unchurched or non-Christian parents. By showing you care about parents' concerns, you'll quickly find them growing more willing to care about your concerns.

PLUGGING PARENTS INTO MINISTRY

Once you have parents "on your team," then what? How can you effectively make them an active part of your youth ministry? Here are 12 no-fail ideas. Use these to help you come up with even more creative ways for parents to "plug in."

1. Special-training leaders. Use parents with specific training skills to lead one-day or weekend workshops for young people. For example, if you have a parent who has experience with horses, ask her to lead a workshop on horseback riding for a small number of kids.

2. Cooks. Ask parents to take turns preparing a snack for your youth group meetings. If they rotate this service, they probably won't have to cook more than two or three times a year. And you won't have to charge kids for refreshments.

3. Trip-meal organizers. Use your parents' shopping skills to organize your trip meals. Have them make out the menu, do comparison shopping, and collect the supplies you'll need. One church that did this changed their average cost of a meal for kids from $5 to $1.50.

4. Supply purchasers. Give a parent a shopping list and ask him or her to do your purchasing for you.

5. Afterglow hosts. Ask parents to host informal get-togethers for your kids after events and meetings (afterglows).

6. Party hosts. Many Sunday school classes have swim parties to kick off the summer season. Have parents who own or have access to swimming pools host these parties.

7. Child-care providers for youth workers. One of the best sources of child care for adults who work with kids is kids' parents.

8. Calligraphers and artists. Parents who are skilled calligraphers or artists can work on your invitations, announcements, and posters.

9. Administrative assistants. If your church can't afford a secretary for you, ask an available parent to "tithe" some time to your ministry by doing paperwork or typing for you.

10. Mother-daughter or father-son retreat coordinators. Many nonchurch organizations hold annual mother-daughter and father-son retreats. Ask a male and female parent to plan them for you.

11. Family event coordinators. Ask a parent to help plan and lead a retreat, picnic, or recreation night that gets families working and playing together.

12. Safe-house volunteers. Tense or abusive situations at home may cause kids to find alternative places to live. Parents can covenant with each other to be available when a young person needs to be out of his or her house.

Finding places where parents can "plug in" and become a part of your ministry is vital to your success with kids. Once all these pieces are in place, you're ready to dig into the nuts and bolts of working with kids on a weekly (and often daily) basis. We'll take a look at how to have effective meetings in Chapter 5.

Constructing Great Meetings

When it comes to building effective meetings for your youth group, you'll be faced with both good news and bad news. The good news is that the second part of this book is crammed with games, crowdbreakers, openers, devotions, and other time-tested ideas that will help you put together a great meeting. (In fact, there are even several already-prepared meetings to get you started on the right track.)

The bad news is that, most of the time, you have to put the elements together piece by piece for each meeting. And that can create problems, because the ingredients you choose and how you arrange them determines the effectiveness of your meetings.

THE BEST APPROACH

When building a youth group meeting, first determine your goal. Is it to have fun? to call for commitment to Christ? to teach a skill or a concept? or to develop unity and relationships? Your goal determines the approach you take.

Second, think through the timing of the meeting *backward.* In other words, begin by deciding what time the meeting should end. Then back up and allow time for the heart of the meeting. For example, if you have a guest speaker, and he or she needs 20 minutes, plan your activities around that nonnegotiable block of time.

As you continue to work backward, make sure all the other parts enhance the heart of the meeting. Ask yourself, "What can be done to best set the stage for the heart of the message?" If your message needs a quiet atmosphere, don't schedule a rip-roaring game just before exploring the message.

Whatever your content vehicle—media, drama, a guest speaker, simulation game, open discussion, role-play, case studies, or debate—make sure the rest of the meeting points to its message. Also, think through how kids might respond. How will the meeting end? How can you reinforce the learning experience at the close?

THE MEETING ELEMENTS

When you're choosing the resources for your next meeting, carefully consider each of these elements.

1. Opening. How you begin sets the tone for the entire meeting. Be enthusiastic, warm, friendly. Let everyone know you're glad they're there and that you're going to have a great time together. The opening also lets everyone know the meeting has started.

2. Games. The purpose of games or crowdbreakers is to have fun and get better acquainted. Use games or activities that tie into the theme of the meeting; for example, a tug of war for them on getting along with parents. Specially chosen music can also reflect the theme and break the ice. Your confidence and enthusiasm will help make games more fun, but beware of games you have to "force" kids to play.

Select appropriate games or crowdbreakers by following these criteria.

● Is the game fun?

● Will kids talk about this tomorrow?

● How does the activity help the group and the meeting?

Begin the meeting with high-energy, total-group involvement. Then move to quieter and more focused activities using small groups or a few students at the front of the room.

3. Experiential "theme" starters. Choose from role-plays, case studies, group projects, instant dramas—any activity that evokes feelings similar to those evoked by the topic you want to study. For example, blindfolding kids and taking them on a "trust walk" evokes emotions that tie in with several issues kids deal with— faith, trust in relationships, the future, leading others to Christ. Activities like this draw kids into the topic and help them "own" their learning process for the rest of the meeting. Read "What Is Active Learning?" on pages 50 and 51 for more information on experiential learning. Also, get a copy of *Do It! Active Learning in Youth Ministry* (Group Publishing) by Thom and Joani Schultz.

4. Discussion or involvement devices. Discussion can be an excellent teaching tool. Discussion gets people involved and helps them think through a concept. But be sure everyone knows why they're having the discussion. Explain that the questions they'll be talking about will help them better understand the meeting's theme.

When planning your discussion, remember these rules.

● Select a subject that's a felt or expressed need. Put yourself in the kids' shoes and test your topic idea by asking, "So what?" or "Why should I care about this?"

● Avoid yes-or-no questions. Always ask, "Why or why not?"

● Be a neutral moderator in the discussion. You can give your viewpoint in the wrap up. But if you do it too soon, you'll stifle discussion by kids who don't want to disagree with your known position. During the discussion, listen politely, accept everyone's comments and ideas, and make sure the discussion moves quickly and stays on track.

5. Life application. Give kids an opportunity to do what they've just been taught or challenged to change. Practice the concepts during the meeting if possible, or if not, draw kids into a commitment to follow through during the week. Hold kids accountable to their commitments by having them pair off and keep tabs on each other's progress, or by organizing a whole-group event where kids live out what they've learned. Remember, they haven't learned it until it becomes a part of their lives.

When planning the commitment part of the meeting, ask:

● Is this doable? Or does it just look good on paper?

What Is Active Learning?

Active learning is, quite simply, learning by *doing*.

In youth ministry, active learning may come to life in something as simple as a foot-washing experience or as exotic as a wilderness adventure week. Active learning may spring from a real-life experience such as a work-camp, or it may stem from a created or simulated experience in a classroom. But however active learning comes, it always exhibits these same seven characteristics.

1. Active learning is an adventure. In active learning, kids may learn lessons the teacher never envisioned. Because the leader trusts students to help create the learning experience, kids may venture into unforeseen discoveries. And often the teacher learns as much as the students.

2. Active learning is fun and/or captivating. Many people assume that fun and learning can't occur at the same time. But if young people find the lesson boring, they probably aren't learning much. Active learning intrigues kids. When students find a foot-washing experience captivating or maybe a bit uncomfortable, they learn. And they often learn on a deeper level than any teacher's lecture alone could reach.

3. Active learning involves everyone. No passive spectators exist in active learning. Everyone must play a part. It's like the difference between watching a football game and playing it with the team. You can learn from both, but you'll learn volumes more and remember it longer if you play along.

4. Active learning is student-based, not teacher-based. Active learning depends on students making discoveries, rather than teachers imparting facts and ideas. Active learning starts with students and moves at their pace. It allows time for unplanned topics to emerge. Though kids may cover less teacher-chosen material, they may actually learn more because of the student-oriented process.

5. Active learning is process-oriented. In active learning, *how* kids arrive at the answer is as important as the answer itself. Focusing on how kids arrive at answers helps them discover the reasons behind the beliefs they have. Then they aren't just following a set of religious rules. They're following Jesus.

6. Active learning is focused through debriefing. Debriefing—or evaluating an experience by discussing in pairs or small groups—helps focus the experience and articulate its application to life. Some good debriefing questions are, "How did this experience make you feel?" "How are those feelings like... (some real-life situation)?" "How can I apply what I've learned in this experience to... (the real-life situation)?"

7. Active learning is relational. Active learning involves personal disclosure on a level most other learning models don't require. Participants are given the opportunity to share openly and honestly about their feelings and their lives. So, active learning has the added benefit of building relationships between individuals and a sense of community in your youth group.

● Will kids be motivated to do this? How?

● Is it a measurable assignment? How can we know it's been accomplished?

UNDER CONSTRUCTION

You now have all the "pieces" of a good meeting. But before you put the parts together for your next meeting, remember these guidelines.

1. Determine your kids' needs; then plan your meetings around those needs.

2. Use variety and creativity, but keep it simple. Your meetings should be fun and lively, but easy to do.

3. Remember, content is most important. Make your lessons "meaty." Your youth group should be more than just another place for kids to go.

4. Model Christian values and teach your kids growth skills.

5. No matter who comes to your meetings, make it worth their while.

Even with the most effectively constructed meetings, things can go wrong. Sometimes you may feel like it would take a bulldozer to prompt your kids to action. We'll take a closer look at trouble-shooting and group dynamics in Chapter 6.

Understanding Group Dynamics

Y ou've researched kids' needs. You've planned a schedule of awesome topics for your youth meetings. You've involved kids in planning and presenting the meetings. You're making the meetings as exciting as you know how.

And they're flopping.

Why? Even the best-planned meetings can go sour, and it often has nothing to do with you or your leadership skills. The problems may be coming from the other major element in your meetings—your kids. It's important to know how to deal with potentially damaging attitudes or behaviors in your youth group long before they get out of hand.

Here's help. Use the tips in this chapter to gain insight into dealing with several common group dynamics problems. Even if you aren't the cause of the problem, you can almost always use your influence to create a solution.

WHEN KIDS DON'T WANT TO BE SERIOUS

Two Rambos in the front row. You noticed them just as you were about to begin the meeting. You could tell they were going to make the evening difficult for you. The one on the left— John—had turned his chair sideways to the others. He straddled it backward. The one on the right—Ron—had that narrow, purposeful look that always precedes mischief.

John and Ron were looking only for fun, not serious discussion. And you're supposed to lead them into a serious encounter with Christ?

By the end of the meeting, the story had changed. They were listening and opening up. Why did you do the make the change? You applied the following four factors to your meeting. Using them helped turn a potential disaster into a special success.

1. Conviction. The human spirit is attracted to conviction. It's repulsed by half-heartedness. Often, kids who don't want to be serious may be trying to send you a coded message: Our youth group lacks conviction. Show us something we can really "buy into."

Conviction is more than enthusiasm or simple belief. It's living passionately for what you believe. You can model conviction in front of your group by "preaching what you practice." In other words, be vulnerable. Let kids see the passion that's in your life because of Christ. Conviction like that catches like wildfire in kids' hearts.

2. Confidence. Confidence is a key to capturing and keeping kids' attention during serious activities. Confidence means you're well-prepared, secure, humble, honest, and not threatened by the other personalities in the room. You can display confidence by realizing that your authority comes from Christ—not from your ability to "control" unruly group members. As kids watch you, set your eyes on Jesus and follow his lead. Rest in the truth that you're the one Jesus has chosen to lead. No one can take that authority away except you.

3. Christ. A convincing, confident environment will draw kids into serious commitment only if the focal point is Christ. Kids rarely get excited about discussing rules and regulations, but they're all too willing to join in a spirited conversation about a relationship—especially if the relationship is with Jesus.

4. Serious-fun checklist. Serious and fun don't have to be opposites. Here's how you can meld the two together.

● Ask yourself before every meeting, "Would this meeting interest me if I were a teenager?"

● Use relational crowdbreakers and activities. These encourage kids to depend on God and each other.

- Create youth group traditions that signal a shift from frivolous to serious. You can do this through a quick song or a phrase you call out, such as "Let's get dangerous!"
- Give disruptive kids special responsibilities in the meeting. If appropriate, ask them to help you lead part of the meeting or create props you use during the meeting.
- Encourage kids' passion for fun. This is so much a part of Jesus' personality. Ecclesiastes 9:10 says, "Whatever work you do, do your best." Join in with kids when they have fun. That will help them join with you when you're serious—and you might learn something about joy in the process.

WHEN KIDS CLAM UP

"Okay everybody, let's get in a circle." The chairs reluctantly scrape into place. "After I read this passage we'll discuss how it applies to school." You read the passage. "I think Paul is saying we need to be patient with ourselves and let Jesus show us his approval of us no matter how we perform. Tori, have you ever been impatient with yourself?"

"Yeah, sometimes." Silence.

"What about you, um, Jeff?" Jeff stares at the floor with a half-smile and nods his head.

Why do they just sit there? How can you draw out teenagers without forcing them to respond? First, understand the reasons kids clam up:

- **emptiness, isolation, and fear.** When you deal with deep topics, sometimes kids think they don't know anything, and conclude they don't have anything valuable to share. They feel alone and doubt their opinions really matter. Being real scares them. And their need for peer approval intensifies this self-consciousness.
- **hints of pretense.** Kids like leaders who don't seem fake. You want to model the Christian life by your actions and words, but sometimes you try too hard. At those times, you might come across as overly spiritual. So kids hesitate to speak up.

● **too deep, too soon.** Starting with a deep, self-revealing subject without warming up to it will stifle communication. Before
asking questions such as "What's the most important thing in your
life?" make sure you've covered lighter ground with questions
such as "If you had to be an insect, which insect would you be
and why?"

After you've pinpointed the reasons why kids aren't talking,
take a look at what you can do to reverse the situation. Evaluate
the following principles to discover how to help kids open up.

1. Make kids comfortable. Do this by being the first to be
transparent and vulnerable. As you disclose your struggles and
imperfections to your group, teenagers will follow your example.
They'll respect your relationship with God more because it's "real"
and not just a bunch of religious hype. And they'll see how God's
love for you could translate into his love for each of them.

Why Guys Rarely Open Up

Why do teenage guys rarely talk
about their feelings? YM magazine
asked 100 guys that question. Here's
how the responses break down:

● They're raised to be strong,
silent, and macho—38%

● They're insecure or afraid of
intimacy—22%

● They *do* talk about their feelings—21%

2. Communicate on kids' level. During discussions, hand the baton of control over to kids. Don't offer your opinion until the end. Most kids enjoy exploring ideas about life, as long as they feel they're safe and respected. So respect kids' opinions. Avoid asking "yes" or "no" questions, and ask lots of questions about how kids feel or what they think. Above all, give kids the right to disagree with you. Don't feel like you have to convince kids of the truth in order to be successful. Even Jesus didn't take on that kind of burden. Your only responsibility is to present the truth clearly. Kids have to decide for themselves whether they'll believe it.

3. Build long-term trust. Understand that openness and vulnerability are byproducts of relationship. Without a foundation of relationship, any success in discussion times will be short-lived at best. Take the time to build relationships with kids in your group outside of the meetings. Especially target those individuals who seem the most hesitant to speak up. They may just be the quiet type. Or they may be waiting to feel "safe" enough to speak out. Give them that safety by building a friendship with them. Once they know you're on their side, they'll find it easier to speak their mind during the meetings.

WHEN ONE GROUP MEMBER BECOMES A WINDBAG

Occasionally every group has a windbag. Someone who seems to do 90 percent of the talking. Someone who drives you up the wall. Someone who blabs on and on. So what can you do about this annoying trait in one of your young people? Consider these ways to handle windbags in your group.

1. Make sure it isn't just you. Try to figure out what you don't like about the windbag. Is it really that he or she talks too much, or do you have some other issue with that person? Find a trusted friend and bounce your impressions off him or her to help you get a handle on what's really bothering you.

2. Don't argue. Windbags usually can't be reasoned with. That's because their goal isn't to win an argument, it's just to keep on arguing. So don't get drawn into a long tirade with one person during a group meeting. Instead, when a windbag takes the group off in a direction you don't like, say, "That's an important point, Susie, and I'll be glad to talk to you about it after the meeting. Right now I want us to stay focused on the meeting topic."

3. Use humor. A windbag may not mind being told to "zip it up" by someone they know, especially if it's done with humor. Humor can take the sting out of blunt messages.

4. Don't let the windbag get control. Plan your meeting so the windbag won't be able to monopolize the conversation. Give the windbag a specific task or a report to make. Use a kitchen timer to limit the length of the reports.

5. Restructure your group. When entering into a discussion time, break off into pairs or small groups and give each person three minutes to share before bringing the groups back together. Windbags aren't so tempted to monopolize in smaller groups, because there's less attention to gain from the effort.

6. Take a direct approach. If all else fails, sit down with the windbag and talk about your feelings and observations. Ask the windbag to use his or her verbal skills to partner with you in facilitating discussion in the group, rather than monopolizing on it.

WHEN NOTHING YOU TRY WORKS

"Nothing I do seems to work with this group. Nothing," said Carol, a youth worker in Pennsylvania. "They think I'm boring. They're rude to me and everyone else. They're ungrateful. They could care less about spiritual things. I've had it. And I'm quitting."

Carol's an outstanding youth leader. Before she led this group, she had successfully led other youth groups for years. But this group was different. Or was Carol different? Sometimes it can be hard to tell.

The fact is that each youth group, like an individual person, has a personality. Some groups are shy, others are outrageous and outgoing. Some groups act as if they've been hurt emotionally, others act rude and stubborn. This last type has been called the "brick-wall" group.

Brick-wall groups foster a pervasive group spirit that's negative, cynical, and sarcastic. No matter what you say or do, kids mock and challenge you. These groups seem to take pride in the number of youth leaders they can force into early retirement.

Do you have a brick-wall group? Gauge your group against these three telltale brick-wall characteristics.

● **The kids are rude.** Of course, not every young person is rude. But the core of the group is rude. You can talk to them repeatedly about courtesy and respect, but it doesn't seem to make any difference.

● **The kids chase others away.** Whenever a young person with a kind and friendly spirit comes into the group, the other group members make it their personal goal to chase the young person away—or convert him or her to a life of rudeness and rebellion.

● **Discipline backfires.** Discipline just doesn't work in a brick-wall group. You can talk to them individually. You can restrict their privileges on youth trips. You can even have the pastor talk to the group. Nothing works.

Does this describe your group? If it does, even a little, you're probably wondering what you did wrong to make the group turn so sour. In fact, it's probably not you at all. Whatever caused your group to grow hard didn't happen last week. It's probably been festering for years.

Here's some of the more common causes of a brick-wall group.

● **Rapid turnover in leadership.** Kids who are constantly being handed from one leader to another get the message that they're not really important to the church or their leaders. They feel rejected and hurt that no one is willing to stick by them. So, as a defense, they decide to reject you before you have the chance to reject them by going away—just like all the other leaders have done.

● **A great history.** Often a brick-wall group had a great group several years ago. But something happened to set the group back, and it hasn't recovered since. Now kids are disillusioned. Underneath their anger, they're feeling worthless and unlovable, because they can't re-create the "good old days."

● **Parents who are active in the church.** If a brick-wall group is composed of mostly strong church families, the bitterness you receive may really be aimed at kids' parents. Kids who are being forced to participate just because Mom and Dad think it's a good idea quickly become bitter and feel that they're not as important to their parents as the church is.

Once you know the reasons for your group's brick-wall nature, what can you do about it? These ideas can help you break down the walls.

1. Deal with the pain. Research your church history to find out the specific cause of your kids' pain. Then, over the next several months, begin to address it. For example, if kids have been shuffled from leader to leader, begin to tell and show kids that you're not going to leave them. When you do this, don't expect them to believe you. They won't—at first. But within a year or two, you'll see a drastic change in the brick-wall nature of your group.

2. Go where the life is. While you're waiting for kids to heal, there will be some kids who are ready to move ahead. Focus a good part of your energy on those kids. Create activities made for smaller groups and take those kids that are willing to go. Let the rest of the group know that you're not rejecting them, but that you need to be doing the things God has called you to do. This sounds hard, but it gives kids a clear choice to make—to stay in their pain or move ahead toward healing.

3. Talk to parents. Meet with parents to discuss your group's problems. Be completely honest about where you believe the harsh attitudes are coming from. Ask parents to help you find creative ways to encourage health in your group.

4. Talk to the key bricks. Who are the cornerstones of your brick-wall group? One way to tell is to ask yourself, "If the group gets noisy, who could tell the group to quiet down and it would listen?" These are the leaders. Pull these kids aside and find out their chief concerns. If you give them the chance, you'll probably find they're surprisingly candid about their feelings.

5. Invite the Holy Spirit to invade your group. Pray consistently for God to bring health into your group. Ask the Holy Spirit to constantly remind you that he's the only true healer—you can't "fix" the group. Only he can.

6. If you decide to leave, don't feel guilty. Leaving doesn't mean you failed. It just means you finished your job. It may be that God called you into the youth group to break down the walls. But breaking walls can leave things looking messy. In the process of healing, some relationships may need to be set aside. In some cases, this could even mean your relationship with kids.

One youth minister decided to leave his brick-wall group after several years of pounding and tearing. Amazing progress had been made, but the residual stress of his relationships with kids was becoming a hindrance to the group's continued health. So he left. Two years later, under new leadership, the group soared from 30 to 60 members. They had evangelistic meetings. They even had a drama team. That youth minister laid the groundwork for all that followed. He knew when his job was done, and he bowed out gracefully.

Healing group hurts isn't an easy or pretty process. But when you're successful, you'll find kids opening up and ready to build relationship with you. We'll talk about how to build one-on-one relationships with kids in the next chapter.

Building Relationships

If you think a guitar, clipboard, and whistle are what make an effective youth leader, toss them aside for a minute. Then read on.

A leader's prime task isn't just to be song leader, organizer, or coach. It's to be a friend to young people. By developing relational skills you model Jesus' love to teenagers.

The first step in modeling Jesus' love is to look at yourself and your relational skills.

YOUR RELATIONAL SKILLS

Use this self-assessment to measure your relational strengths and weaknesses.

1. Remember when. Get in touch with who influenced your development of relational skills.

● Think of an adult you knew during your teenage years who related to you in positive ways. Jot down what you remember about this person. Why does this person come to mind now?

● Think of another adult from your early years who didn't relate to you well. Write why you thought about this person now.

● In what ways have people shared their faith with you? Note ways that are especially helpful, and why.

2. Consider your gifts. List your relational gifts. Here are some gifts to get you started. Check the ones God's given to you.

_____ listening

_____ caring for others in personal ways

_____ being available

_____ smiling

_____ saying positive things to and about others

_____ being an advocate for young people

_____ telling others Jesus' story

Now list gifts you have that aren't mentioned above.

If possible, talk about these two lists with someone. Let them help you think of other relational gifts you have developed.

3. Devise a wish list. List five gifts you wish you had when it comes to relating to others. This helps you focus on skills you may want to develop.

I wish I had the gifts of:

Prioritize your "wish list" from 1 to 5. For the next month, work on developing priority 1. After that, work on priority 2, and so on. By next year, your wish list will be transformed into your gift list.

JESUS AS A RELATIONAL MODEL

Now that you've gotten a better idea of yourself and your skills, focus on God's ideas.

"This is what real love is: It is not our love for God; it is God's love for us" (1 John 4:10a). Because God made the first move and loved you through Christ's death and resurrection, you're called to develop relationships with others. You're not asked to relate to young people only on a human level—being nice, helping with problems, giving your time. You're also called by God to relate the Lord's power—praying, faith-sharing, being concerned with spiritual growth. Relationships begin with sharing faith through your lifestyle.

When it comes to relating to kids, Jesus is the best model. Do what Jesus did. He took time to listen, touch, give, care, reach out—all examples for friendly interaction with teenagers.

And more than Jesus' model of love, he forgives. His forgiveness packs the power that enables you to relate to young people—even when you don't listen enough, smile enough, or share enough.

Recall how Jesus related to different people in different ways. Notice he spent time with his closest friends, the disciples. He equipped them to care for and love others.

A LEADER'S SERVANT ROLE

In all of his relationships, Jesus served. So, relational leaders are servants first. Check out Mark 10:42-45. "The Son of Man did not come to be served. He came to serve others and to give his life as a ransom for many people" (Mark 10:45). You as a leader certainly have power. But power is safe only in the hands of those who humble themselves to serve others. A servant leader sees people first, programs second. A servant youth leader sees the needs, hopes, joys, and pains of kids first. And then, in dealing with individuals, a servant leader develops strategies that respond to the needs.

THE S.O.F.T.E.N APPROACH

You can be a servant who follows Christ's example. It's not hard when you use the S.O.F.T.E.N approach. It stands for smiles, openness, forwardness, touch, eye contact, and nodding.

1. Smiles. It's no surprise. People who relate well with others smile, and share their attitude of joy and celebration.

2. Openness. Relational people demonstrate more availability and more openness to listening and speaking with others.

3. Forwardness. Relational people are positive and assertive in their approaches to others. They seek out people to talk with; they watch for the lonely; they're sensitive to others' feelings.

4. Touch. Relational people effectively use touch. Appropriate touch—a handshake, hug, pat on the back, squeeze of the elbow—shows others you care. Be careful not to overpower others. Comfortable touch develops as you and group members grow to know each other better.

5. Eye contact. Relational leaders maintain good eye contact. That tells people "I care, I'm listening, tell me more!"

6. Nodding. Relational people use nods to let people know they're listening. Nodding encourages the person who's talking.

As you continue your friendships with young people, practice doing these things.

1. Ask for help. Don't try to develop your relational skills without feedback from others. For example, choose others to help you develop your listening skills. Ask trusted friends to hold you accountable to become a better listener. Request evaluations and constructive criticism. Then move toward improvement.

2. Take advantage of opportunities for growth. For instance, on a retreat, make a covenant with yourself that you'll get to know three young people better during the weekend. Then work at it.

3. Attend educational events. Sign up for opportunities to study communication skills or understanding teenagers. Learn how to more effectively meet kids' needs.

4. Read relational-type materials. Some good resources include *Counseling Teenagers* by Keith Olson (Group), *Building Community in Youth Groups* and *Youth Group Trust Builders* by Denny Rydberg (Group), and *Bringing Out the Best in People* by Alan Loy McGinnis, author of *The Friendship Factor* (HarperCollins).

5. Watch yourself. Pay attention to your actions when you relate to others. What do they see? Do you talk more than you listen? How are you communicating your genuine interest?

6. Ask role models for advice. If you have a mentor or model, ask this person to help you develop relational skills. Practice by role playing. Do communication exercises, or act out typical youth group situations or confrontations.

7. Study scripture. Continue to check out Jesus' style, and model the way he loved and cared for others.

8. Be ready to forgive. This includes yourself as well as others. When you fall short of relating to people, when you get angry at yourself for something you said in haste, be assured you're forgiven in Christ. He gives you the power to start over again!

9. Observe others. Watch others communicate. Check out certain "likable" styles and gifts. Borrow those ideas and patterns

Five Friendship Skills for Leaders

A relational leader needs a positive self-image to create a sense of confidence in others. One survey of 90 business leaders uncovered these five skills needed in developing relationships. Circle the number that best indicates your skill-level in each area—1 is strong; 6 is weak.

1. The ability to accept people as they are, not as you'd like them to be.

1   2   3   4   5   6

2. The ability to approach relationships and problems in terms of the present rather than the past.

1   2   3   4   5   6

3. The ability to treat people close to you with the same courteous attention you extend to strangers.

1   2   3   4   5   6

4. The ability to trust others, even when the risk seems great.

1   2   3   4   5   6

5. The ability to do without constant approval and recognition from others.

1   2   3   4   5   6

Gather with your ministry leadership team and discuss the implications of these five leadership areas. Do you disagree with any of them? agree? Why? Would you add any other skills? If so, what?

you can effectively incorporate into your own communication style without compromising your personality.

10. Don't panic. Don't set yourself up for failure by assuming it's easy to develop relational skills. It isn't. Give yourself time. And be realistic. Your goal isn't to become "great communicator" of the century. You just want to reach your full potential as an individual. That's all God asks.

Once you begin to deepen your relationships with young people, they'll start opening up to you about the real-life struggles they face. As their leader, kids will be looking to you for comfort and guidance. You need to know how to counsel kids in crisis. Let's look at how to do that in the next chapter.

CHAPTER 8

Counseling

"**N**ot the kids in my group," interrupted the confident youth pastor.

The youth ministry seminar leader paused briefly, and then continued. "Several national studies reveal that half or more of America's teenagers have had sexual intercourse by age 18."

The confident youth pastor in the back row stood up. "You must be talking about a completely different bunch of kids," he argued. "These figures don't represent kids in my church. And I don't think they represent the kids in most church youth groups. We're dealing with Christian kids—church kids—not a bunch of immoral sinners off the street. Talk to us about *our* kids!"

"Okay, you asked for it," the seminar leader said. "A research organization did a study of active church youth group members in the Midwest. Their finding showed that 42 percent of the girls and 59 percent of the guys experience sexual intercourse by age 18."

"Well, they didn't survey my kids," the youth pastor retorted, still unconvinced.

NO IMMUNITY IN THE CHURCH

Attending church doesn't make kids immune from the problems that plague society. Being Christian doesn't spare people from stumbling.

National statistics on trends among young people deserve our close attention. Of course, no national trend will be duplicated precisely in your youth group. Your group is unique; your kids will differ somewhat from national surveys. But we tread on dangerous ground when we categorically ignore all national data because we believe our kids are so different. Our kids may differ somewhat from the national average, but the problems that affect society as a whole also affect those who walk through our church doors.

TRENDS TO WATCH

Church young people—even younger teenagers—are sexually active. In fact, Search Institute found that 26 percent of a predominantly churched sample of eighth-grade guys reported experience with sexual intercourse. As we talk with young people about sexuality, we must be sensitive to those who may already be dealing with guilt, confusion, or shame.

Search Institute also uncovered statistics on drug and alcohol use among our churches' young teenagers. For example, 53 percent of the ninth-graders used alcohol during the preceding year, and 28 percent reported getting drunk during the last year.

Marijuana was used by 20 percent of the kids. Obviously, our youth group members could use some guidance on chemical abuse. Other trends affecting our young people:

● **Divorce**—One in four families with children lives in a single-parent household.

● **Eating disorders**—At least 10 to 15 percent of all teenage girls struggle with some form of eating disorder.

● **Sexual abuse**—One in three females is sexually abused before she reaches the age of 18. At least one in eight males suffers the same fate.

Today's young people face a web of adolescent problems. We must never be so naive as to assume our church kids are somehow immune.

Before you can begin to understand how to counsel effectively with kids who carry around issues like the ones mentioned above, you have to discover the root problem. Teaching a girl to stop throwing up after every meal might solve her surface problem. But she won't be truly healthy until you've helped her uncover her root issues, and invite Jesus to come and heal her heart.

Root problems usually stem from root relationships. Root relationships are those relationships each of us has that largely shape who we are. These relationships include mom, dad, brothers, sisters, or any other significant adult or relative from our childhood experience. Root problems occur when something goes wrong in one of our root relationships. A father becomes alcoholic. A mother neglects her children. An uncle sexually molests his sister's son. A brother dies. All of these situations (and many others like them) send destructive waves into a child's developmental process. If those problems aren't handled quickly and sensitively, they fester and grow until a child becomes incapable of dealing effectively with real life. When this happens, kids go into a "survival" mode. They find ways to get through life, whatever it takes. The results: kids giving in to drugs or alcohol, moving into a homosexual lifestyle, becoming chained to an eating disorder, even becoming abusive or violent.

HELPING KIDS FIND HEALING

For a young person who's struggling with alcohol, telling him to "just stop it" won't really help. In fact, it will hurt. We need to recognize that the alcohol problem (or any other "outside" problem) is just a signal beacon alerting you to deeper, root problems underneath. In counseling, the first rule of healing is, "You have to look backward in order to move ahead." In other words, help kids trace their present problems back to the root cause, even if it seems totally unrelated. Almost always, this means taking a look at root relationships.

Michael skips school a lot. When he's in school, he often winds up in the principal's office. Michael doesn't have many friends.

You suspect Michael uses drugs. And you feel sad for his parents. His dad is a longtime lay leader at your church, and his mother is respected for her community work.

Then there's Gerry. He's your idea of the perfect teenager. He packs his schedule with baseball practice, play rehearsal, band practice, debate-club tournaments, and student-government meetings. On weekends he works at McDonald's. Although his parents never come to church, he's a leader in your youth group. Everyone likes him.

It's obvious Michael needs help. But what's hard to believe is that Gerry needs the same kind of help Michael does. Both Michael and Gerry come from dysfunctional families. But what kind of family is dysfunctional? What are the warning signs? How can you counsel kids from dysfunctional families when they act so differently?

Dysfunctional families don't all look the same. But a family is dysfunctional when it fails to meet the deepest relational needs of its members. Individual family members are hurt, some nearly hopelessly, when unconditional love and nurturing aren't supplied in the home. A family breaks down when its members search elsewhere for these essential ingredients to adult health. Kids will search for these missing elements in other people. But when their search meets with failure, they turn to other substitutes such as sex, drugs, food, or a whole host of other survival behaviors.

HOW CAN I HELP?

Counseling kids about applying themselves in school, comforting a guy when a girl dumps him, talking to a teenager about deepening her commitment to God—all of these fall within the realm of "normal" counseling situations that you'll face in your youth group. But what should you do when larger problems surface? How do you balance your concern for the young person with your need to support the parents? How can you help kids deal with these deeper problems without getting yourself caught in the middle of a family cross fire? Try these suggestions.

1. Redefine "healthy family." It's easy to judge a family by the traditional basic functions we've all come to look for—protection, economic security, education, religious training, and status. Church workers tend to use this old standard more regularly than other family workers. So, in order to recognize dysfunctional traits in kids, you need to redefine your view of what makes a family healthy. See the "Healthy Family Traits" box on page 74 to get you started on revamping the way you view family health.

2. Understand co-dependence. Co-dependence is a risk in any family characterized by denial of reality, compulsive behavior, and emotional repression. Check out your local bookstore for a good resource on the effects and signs of co-dependence. Watch for these signs in your group members.

3. Refer kids to professionals. Both Michael and Gerry need more help than your training likely allows. Refer them to an agency, group, or therapist who works with dysfunctional families and their co-dependent members. Your local Alcoholics Anonymous group should be able to direct you to such resources.

4. Model healthy relationships. Start with the "Healthy Family Traits" on page 74. By applying these traits to your group, you'll provide a haven for kids from dysfunctional homes and a nurturing place for all your kids.

5. Encourage hope in Jesus. Kids from dysfunctional families survive largely on hope. Their enemy is despair, and they fight it through denial and emotional repression. But for all these kids, hope in anything other than Jesus will end in disillusionment. Present Jesus to your kids as the only true source of hope in life and encourage kids to risk trusting him with their pain.

Learning how to handle different types of counseling situations will help you balance your desire to "fix" kids' problems with their realistic needs. You'll learn when to dig in and help kids work through their issues, and when to refer kids to counselors with more training. In Chapter 9, we'll look at a broader "balancing" issue—the balance between your ministry and your personal life.

Healthy Family Traits

What makes a family healthy? Dolores Curran identifies 15 family strengths in her book *Traits of a Healthy Family*. A healthy, functional family

- communicates and listens,
- affirms and supports one another,
- teaches respect for others,
- develops trust,
- has a sense of play and humor,
- exhibits shared responsibility,
- teaches right and wrong,
- has rituals and traditions that abound,
- has a balance of interaction among members,
- has a shared religious core,
- respects the privacy of one another,
- values service to others,
- fosters family table time and conversation,
- shares leisure time, and
- admits to and seeks help with problems.

CHAPTER 9

Balancing Your Life and Ministry

Read the following real-life story of one youth worker. See how much of yourself you see in him.

"In my first youth ministry job, I started working the first day and didn't stop. Youth group attendance rose from eight to more than 50 during the first three months. We organized paper drives, lock-ins, prayer breakfasts, and a retreat where more than 100 kids showed up.

"The community loved me. I went to football games, basketball games, wrestling meets, soccer games, school dances, and choir concerts. I met parents and teachers. I called meetings.

"Then one morning six months into the job, I couldn't get out of bed. I felt too tired. When I finally climbed out of bed, I went to my office, locked the door, and read the newspaper. Work sat in stacks. Programs waited to be planned. Lesson plans begged for outlines. But I just couldn't do anything.

"Then I realized that during those six months, I hadn't spent a single uninterrupted day with my family. I hadn't read a book. I hadn't seen a movie. I had only watched the news on television before falling asleep in my chair."

Balancing your life and ministry can be tricky business. But like this youth worker discovered, when ministry takes precedence over higher priorities in life, everything suffers—*including* your ministry. Your personal relationship with God and with your family is more important than keeping your ministry afloat. And, if you don't get those priorities in order, your whole life could go up in smoke.

How do you avoid destruction? How do you balance your personal life and your ministry? Follow these eight steps as insurance against becoming overcommitted to your ministry.

1. Take time off. Schedule one day each week when you don't go into the office at all. Trust your colleagues to handle things for one day. Guard that day with vigilance. Don't allow any situation to impose itself on your life that day unless it's a life or death emergency. Then, once you've established that day as "off limits" to others, decide what you'll do with your newly found free time. It could be anything, so long as it's totally nonwork related.

2. Plan a vacation. Vacations don't plan themselves. They take time, money, and work if you're going to do them right.

First, decide what kind of vacation you need. Some people prefer several short vacations a year rather than one long one. Others like to take off once and be gone for at least two weeks.

Whichever kind suits you, start planning for it early. Anticipation is half the fun, and the thought of lying on the beach can get you through some pretty tough times. Collect brochures. Start a savings jar for your loose change. All this extends the vacation and keeps you going.

But whatever you do, don't make the horrible mistake of staying home. Go away. Leave your church responsibilities in the hands of someone you trust, and get away. Those "stay home" vacations rarely work.

3. Hang out with your friends. Friends inside and outside the church can help you take care of yourself and your family. Real friends let you be yourself. They understand how you feel.

Do you want your friends to feel important? Don't take calls while you're spending time with them—no matter who they're from.

Cultivate friendships where you jog, bowl, eat out; cultivate friendships in your neighborhood. Most importantly, cultivate friendships outside your youth group leadership team. That way, when you need to "get away" from the church, you'll have someplace to go.

4. Learn new ideas. People who are feeling burned out often feel empty as well. They've used up all their ideas. They've said everything they have to say on the subject. And they often feel like they're the only ones who feel this way.

Continuing education places new input, ideas, insights, data, and probably most important, new people in the picture. Continuing education events provide you with opportunities to network with people from across the country who share your interests.

New, exciting, ground-breaking things are being done and discovered all the time. But you won't find out about them if you stop trying to learn.

Reading youth ministry publications isn't enough. Sponsor events in your church. Or save money and attend one that's in a far-off place. If you don't have much money, check your church budget. Often churches set aside funds for staff member education.

5. Find a hobby. Take time each day to do something for yourself. You need to take care of yourself if you want to take care of others.

Read the newspaper. Take a nap. Drink a cup of sassafras tea. Eat an ice cream cone. Work out. Do a crossword puzzle. Style your hair. It doesn't have to be something big; it just needs to be something for you.

6. Pamper your family. You can't recapture the big days in your children's lives if you let those days slip away. Birthdays, school programs, Little League games, PTA meetings—they're all important. And they deserve your time and attention.

Write these events on your calendar early and leave plenty of time to get there and get home afterward. Don't let your children believe they're less important than your ministry.

Plan time alone with your spouse. Eat a long lunch together. Go away for a weekend. Sit in a mall and watch people together. Wake up 30 minutes earlier than usual and read the newspaper to each other. Read a book together. Or just talk.

Jobs come and go, but a family lasts forever. Take care of those relationships, and they'll take care of you when life gets tough.

7. Take care of your health. A person who's too busy to eat right is too busy. Listen to your body when it talks to you. Eat right. Get plenty of rest. Exercise. Letting yourself get too heavy or

Life-Balance Quiz

Answer "yes" or "no" to the following questions to see how well you balance your life and ministry. Then total your responses.

_____ 1. Your best friend calls and asks you to attend a basketball game. You haven't seen your friend in a while, but you don't really like basketball, and you have some work to do for church. Would you go?

_____ 2. Do you read scriptures daily and read at least one other book each month that has nothing to do with your ministry directly?

_____ 3. Have you attended at least one seminar or training session within the last year that will enhance your ability as a youth leader?

_____ 4. Do you keep up with current events?

_____ 5. Do you work out vigorously at least three times a week?

_____ 6. Do you volunteer for community activities not related to your church?

_____ 7. Are you presently pursuing any hobbies?

_____ 8. If you have children, do you spend an hour of uninterrupted time with them each day? If you don't have children, do you spend an hour of uninterrupted time each day doing something you personally value?

_____ 9. Do you eat right?

_____ 10. If you're married, do you go on at least two "dates" each month with your spouse? If you're not married, do you go out at least twice a month with friends, just to have fun?

_____ 11. At least once a year, do you think about your future and evaluate your direction in life?

_____ 12. Do you spend quiet "down time" alone at least twice a week?

Total "yes" _____

Total "no" _____

Use these scores to see how well-balanced your life is.

9 to 12 "yes"—You're doing an excellent job of keeping your life in balance.

6 to 8 "yes"—You're doing a fair job, but you can still improve.

3 to 5 "yes"—You have a poor balance in your life and you need to get back on track.

0 to 2 "yes"—Your life is totally unbalanced. Today's the day to begin to make some important changes.

too thin is unfair to you, your family, and your ministry. You can't perform your youth ministry well if you don't feel well physically. Your body is an important ministry tool. Take care of it.

8. Spend lots of time with God. Recognize the ultimate value of your most important relationship and give time to it accordingly. This doesn't mean you have to spend hours studying Bible commentaries or that you have to learn Hebrew. Remember, Jesus is a person. Spend time with him. Go on bike rides together. Take a trip alone with him. Talk to him frequently throughout the day. Listen to him. The Holy Spirit will be as present as you allow him to be. Remember, he loves you. It's his greatest heart's desire to spend time with you. Believe it and start getting to know the God who died to have the chance to get to know you.

Part 2:
No-Fail Ideas
for Youth Ministry

CHAPTER 10

Meetings

Different kids learn differently. If you use only one learning style in your lessons, you're making it hard for some of your kids to get the point.

Psychologist Howard Gardner has identified seven learning styles.

● Linguistic—learning by hearing or reading words (kids who love book studies and devotionals).

● Logical-Mathematical—learning through concepts or "mental equations" (kids who respond to things like "The Four Spiritual Laws").

● Spatial—learning through images (kids who learn best through object lessons).

● Musical—learning through sounds (kids who are die-hard members of the youth choir).

● Kinesthetic—learning through movements (kids who find profound meaning in active games or programs).

● Interpersonal—learning through interactions with people (kids who volunteer to be on your social task forces).

● Intrapersonal—learning by introspection and alone time (kids who hunger for more quiet, alone time on retreats).

Think about your kids. Now think about your ministry and the way you conduct your meetings. Ask yourself, "Am I meeting the learning needs of my kids?" Consider all the learning styles as you use these ready-made meeting outlines with your kids. And plan future meetings to incorporate learning experiences that attract all kinds of learners, not just some.

MEETING 1: FINDING GOD'S PEACE IN LIFE'S STORMS

Use this Bible study to show kids God's full plan for finding peace.

OBJECTIVES
In this Bible study kids will
- experience anxiety,
- identify things that cause anxiety,
- discover God's six-step plan for finding peace, and
- determine ways to find peace in their lives.

BEFORE THE BIBLE STUDY
For activity 1, write each of the following instructions on separate slips of paper, "Bump into others and fall down," "Sing a song using the wrong notes," "Call out, 'Please, someone help me!' " "Act depressed," "Treat people with impatience," and "Worry out loud." You'll need a slip of paper for each group member.

For activity 3, blow up and tie off two balloons. Cut a 2-inch slit into the 3-inch side of two 3×5 cards and insert the tied end of a balloon into the slit in each card. Draw a face on each balloon. The 3×5 cards serve as "feet" for the balloons.

Read the Bible study, collect the supplies, and photocopy the handouts.

THE BIBLE STUDY
1. Opener: High Anxiety—(You'll need the slips of paper prepared beforehand.) Welcome kids, and then say: **Today we're going to act out some anxiety-producing situations. Then we'll discover God's six-step plan for handling our worries— a plan for finding God's peace.**

Give each person a slip of paper with an instruction. For two minutes, have kids act out their instructions.

PEACE

Shalom!
(Philippians 4:1-7)

Make your
worries known
to God
(verses 6-7)

Operate with patient
endurance (verse 5)

Live it up! Rejoice! (verse 4)

Assist others (verse 3)

Harmonize together—agree with one another (verse 2)

Stand firm in the Lord (verse 1)

Afterward, ask: **How did you feel as you acted out your instructions? How did others' actions make you feel? When did you feel anxious?**

2. Help! Thief!—(You'll need paper, pencils, and Bibles.) Say: **Each of the actions in the opening activity illustrates a potential threat to peace. Let's examine thieves of peace more closely.**

Form two teams. Give each team a Bible, paper, and pencils. Have teams read Philippians 4:1-7. Ask them to look for things in each verse that God says could cause anxiety. For example, verse 2 indicates that disagreement can cause anxiety.

Have teams write as many thieves of peace as they can think of on separate sheets of paper. For example, teams might write, "A fight with friends," "I'm worried about not having enough money," or "Flunking a test."

After five minutes, have teams each read their peace thieves. After each peace thief is read, have team members wad the paper and keep the paper wads for the next activity.

3. Standing Firm—(You'll need the two balloons prepared beforehand, masking tape, and the peace thieves paper wads.) Move the furniture to the edge of the room. Set the prepared balloons in the middle of the room. Tape a line 5 feet away from each side of the balloons. Have each team bring its pile of peace thieves paper wads and stand on a line.

Say: **God's goal is for us to stand firm in his peace. But peace thieves often rob us of God's peace. In this game, your goal is to use your paper peace thieves to keep these balloon "people" from standing firm. The team that moves its balloon person farthest away from where it is now is the winner. You must stand on your line at all times.**

Designate which balloon belongs to which team, and say "go." Afterward, declare the winner. Then ask: **How did you feel as you bombarded your balloon person? How does it feel when you're bombarded with real peace thieves? What do you do when your peace is stolen?**

4. Peace Talks—(You'll need a Bible.) Form pairs. Give each pair three minutes to define "peace." Call time. Ask one volunteer from each pair to stand. One by one, have each volunteer tell the definition and sit. Encourage volunteers to sit if someone tells a definition that's similar to their own. Continue to look for new ways of defining peace until everyone is sitting.

Say: **Although these are good definitions of peace, the Bible says that God's peace "is so great we can't understand it."**

Read aloud Philippians 4:6-7. Ask: **How many of you have heard these verses before this meeting? How many of you have ever read or quoted these verses to someone who needed peace? What does this scripture passage mean?**

Say: **Prayer is just one of the many steps God gives us to find his peace. Let's look at each of God's steps to peace.**

5. Peace on Earth—(For each person you'll need a photocopy of the "Shalom" illustration on page 85. You'll also need three Bibles and three copies of the "War Zone" handout on page 88.) Give each group member a photocopy of the "Shalom" illustration. Say: **"Shalom" is a Hebrew word that means peace. Jewish people and people in Arab countries often greet each other with the word "shalom." We're going to use this word to teach us more about God's peace.**

Form six groups. A group can be one person. Assign each group a stair step from the "Shalom" acrostic. Have each group read aloud its verse and discuss why that step is important to finding God's peace. Have a volunteer from each group report the group's discoveries. For example, verse 4 says to rejoice. Happiness and thankfulness remind us of God's blessings and help us forget our worries.

Place a Bible and a "War Zone" handout in each of three locations around the room. Declare these three locations land mines 1, 2, and 3. Assign two groups to each land mine and have them sit down.

Say: **We've now entered a war zone. You're each strategically positioned near a land mine—or an explosive, peace-stealing situation. Your group must read your land-mine situation from the "War Zone" handout, read the Bible verse that goes with it, and then use God's six-step peace plan to decide how you'd defuse that land mine in order to reach peace.**

For example, to handle anxiety-producing land mine 1, kids could stand firm in their knowledge that God loves them and has

WAR ZONE

Follow these directions:

■ Read your assigned land-mine situation.

■ Read the scripture to gain other insight.

■ Use the six-step peace plan to decide how to deal with that land mine in order to reach God's peace.

Land mine 1: The world seems out of control. There's so much war, violence and crime. It's a scary place to live (John 14:27).

Land mine 2: Youth group members can't agree on where to go on a missions trip. Some kids are getting angry about it (Romans 12:18).

Land mine 3: Everything seems to be going wrong in your family. Your parents fight with each other. Your brother and sister bicker about everything. You're tired of all the yelling (Ephesians 4:31-32).

overcome the world. Although the world seems out of control, they can still harmonize with their friends and relatives, and assist others who are in need. They can count their blessings and be happy that God has given them so much—patiently enduring the scary times knowing that God is in control. And they can pray about their worries—God will give them peace.

Give kids five minutes at their assigned land mines. Then signal them to rotate clockwise to the next land mine. Allow five minutes for groups to work through this new land mine, and then have them rotate one final time.

After group members have worked through each land mine, ask: **How did your group handle each explosive situation? How is each of these six steps necessary to find God's peace? Which step would be most difficult for you when your peace is threatened? Explain.**

6. Closing: Peaceful Resort—(You'll need fruit, healthy cookies, or other goodies.) Say: **Congratulations! You entered a war zone and worked out peaceful solutions to peace-stealing problems.**

Serve goodies as rewards for group members' successful peace pursuits. As kids are enjoying their snacks, say: **The Bible says to let our requests be made known to God with prayer and supplication. It's important when we're troubled to ask God humbly and earnestly to help us. Let's do that now.**

Form pairs. Have partners each tell one thing that's threatening to steal their peace. Let them work through God's six-step plan to find peace in their situations. Then have partners pray for each other to take the appropriate steps to find God's peace.

Encourage group members to take home their "Shalom" illustrations as reminders of ways to seek God's peace.

Use this no-more-excuses Bible study to challenge kids to share their faith.

OBJECTIVES
In this Bible study kids will
● recognize the obstacles to faith-sharing,
● see how a group of friends in the Bible overcame obstacles to bring their friend to Jesus,
● discover new ways to overcome obstacles to faith-sharing, and
● create a new tool to use in faith-sharing.

BEFORE THE BIBLE STUDY
Read the Bible study and collect supplies. Design an obstacle course (see the "Obstacle Course Example" page 93 for ideas). Use masking tape to outline on the floor rivers with stepping stones. You can use paper plates for stepping stones. Chairs can be used as barriers or obstacles. Tables can be used as mountains or bridges—to go over or under. A taped square can represent the hospital.

THE BIBLE STUDY
1. Opener: Medic Race—(You'll need stretchers, blankets or sleeping bags, a watch with a second hand, Dr. Pepper soft drinks, and a prepared obstacle course.) Form teams with no more than five on each team. Designate one "wounded" person per team who'll ride on the "stretcher." Safety is important to this activity, so designate a spotter for each team.

Say: **You're about to compete in a Medic Race. Your team's objective is to transport your wounded person to the hospital in the least amount of time. But if you drop your wounded person, your team is disqualified and out of the race.**

Show teams the proper path through the obstacle course (they must use the "stones" in the river to get across). Have teams start one at a time. When the first team is halfway through the obstacle course, have the second team start. Stagger the teams until all teams have run the obstacle course. Time each team. Award a Dr. Pepper to each person on the team with the best time.

Don't straighten up the room yet. The obstacle course will serve as a constant visual reminder.

Ask: **Which was the easiest obstacle in the Medic Race? Which obstacle presented the biggest challenge? What's a new and creative way your team overcame an obstacle? How did you feel as your team overcame obstacles? Have you ever had to face obstacles in sharing your faith with someone? If so, what were the obstacles and how did you try to overcome them?**

2. Bible Study: Breaking Through the Roof—(You'll need a Bible, newsprint, a marker, and tape.) Read aloud Mark 2:1-12.

Ask: **How is Jesus like a hospital in the story? Would you have done what the four friends did for their friend in the story? Why or why not? What are the different obstacles the four friends had to face in getting the paralytic to Jesus?**

Write kids' answers to the "obstacle" question on newsprint taped to a wall. Then add to their list, if necessary, by talking about these obstacles:

● Distance—By the time the four friends arrived with the paralytic, the house was full and even the doorway was completely filled.

● People—The only real obstacle to Jesus was people. So many people were around Jesus, but no one moved or tried to help the paralytic. Only the four friends sacrificed for him.

● The roof—Most homes at that time were made of stone and had stairs to the roof. It must've been difficult to get the stretcher to the roof.

● Breaking through the roof—Most people would've stopped when they saw the crowd, but these four friends were determined enough to create a hole in the roof.

Ask: **Why did the friends work so hard to get their friend to Jesus? What was the greatest obstacle they had to overcome? Explain. Do you think it's any easier today to bring people to Jesus? Why or why not?**

91

3. Obstacle-Busters—(You'll need newsprint, markers, tape, balloons, paper, and pencils.) Write, "Obstacles to Faith-Sharing," on a sheet of newsprint and tape it to a wall. Give kids each a marker. Allow five minutes for kids to write on the newsprint the obstacles they face in telling others about their faith in Christ. Afterward, ask kids to explain the obstacles they wrote.

Then ask the group to vote on the top five obstacles they face.

Blow up five balloons. Use a marker to write each of the top five obstacles on a balloon and on a separate sheet of newsprint. Form five groups and assign each one an obstacle. Have groups each brainstorm ways to overcome their assigned obstacle, and then write those ways on their newsprint. Then have a volunteer from each group read aloud his or her group's obstacle-busters.

Challenge groups to each use their obstacle-buster newsprint to pop the appropriate obstacle balloon. Kids may use only the newsprint to pop the balloon. For example, kids might roll the newsprint into a spear and pop the balloon. (This sounds impossible, but it works.)

After all the balloons are popped, say: **It's not easy, but we can overcome the obstacles we face in telling others about Christ. Just as you worked hard to pop the balloons, we may have to work hard to overcome the obstacles to faith-sharing.**

Give kids in each group a sheet of paper and a pencil. Tell kids to each write on the paper their #1 obstacle to telling others about Christ. Then have the groups each develop an action plan for each group member to use in overcoming his or her obstacle.

4. Taking Detours—(You'll need paper, posterboard, markers, magazines, glue, tape, scissors, and a Bible.) Form groups of three. Give each group paper, posterboard, markers, magazines, glue, tape, and scissors.

Say: **Many of our friends are like the paralytic we read about earlier. They have hurts and problems only Jesus can heal. If we let the obstacles stand in our way, we may never bring them to Jesus. We're going to do an experiment in telling others about our faith in Christ.**

Read aloud John 3:16-17. Have groups each brainstorm what's important for their friends to know about a relationship with Christ. Then tell groups to each create a faith-sharing tool using the mate-

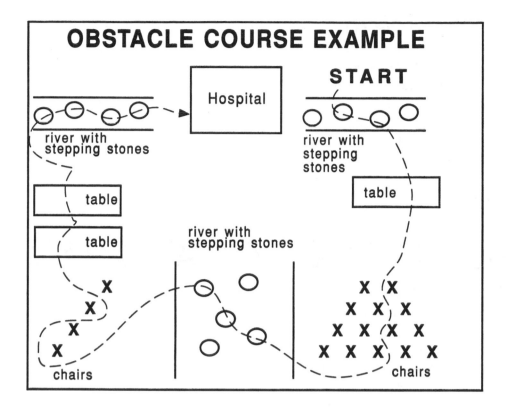

OBSTACLE COURSE EXAMPLE

Hospital

START

river with stepping stones

river with stepping stones

table

table

river with stepping stones

chairs

chairs

rials you gave them for each person in their group to use in telling their friends about Jesus. They could make a pamphlet, poster, collage, or flier. Encourage kids to be creative. Be sure kids understand they're actually going to use their faith-sharing tool.

Challenge kids to think about how they'll use their faith-sharing tool with a friend. Be available to groups if they need help.

After groups are finished with their creations, have them each choose one person in their group to act out the role of a non-Christian. Have groups each take three minutes to role play the two Christians using their faith-sharing tool with their non-Christian friend. Encourage kids to use their faith-sharing tool with a non-Christian friend this week.

5. Closing: Action Prayer—(You'll need each group's action plan from the "Obstacle-Busters" activity.) Form a circle and have kids hold hands. One at a time, have kids each read aloud their action plan from the "Obstacle-Busters" activity. As kids each read aloud their action plan, have the person on their right pray for them to overcome their obstacles to faith-sharing this week. Then ask the person who read aloud to stand outside of the circle. Continue around the circle, going right, until everyone is outside of the circle. The first person out of the circle should pray for the last person in the circle.

Then tell kids to race to straighten up the room and the obstacle course in one minute. You may want to allow more time, if you have a small group. When all obstacles are removed, have kids run back, form a circle and yell "amen!"

MEETING 3: EVERYTHING TO LIVE FOR!

Use this meeting to help your teenagers see the choices they have—life or death—and to choose life.

OBJECTIVES

In this Bible study kids will
- experience the frustration of failure,
- identify feelings associated with suicide,
- compare and contrast the lives of Simon Peter and Judas Iscariot,
- develop counseling tools for suicidal friends, and
- affirm their individual uniqueness.

BEFORE THE BIBLE STUDY

Read the Bible study, collect supplies, and photocopy the handouts.

THE BIBLE STUDY

1. Opener: Paper Houses—(You'll need tape, paper, and a book.) Form groups of four. Give each group tape and several sheets of paper. Allow 10 minutes for groups to each create a paper house that is at least 4 feet high. Encourage groups to build for strength.

Afterward, say: **Your houses reflect people's lives. Some are tall and straight. Others are slightly lopsided. And a few could**

94

use a little more help. (Draw other analogies as appropriate.)

Now place a book on each house to "test" its strength. Most will fail this test. Praise houses that pass the test.

Ask: **How did you feel as you built your house? How did you feel when your house did or didn't pass the strength test? What building materials would've made it stronger? If your life is like this house, what pressures can cause your life to cave in? What can you do to strengthen your life to withstand these pressures?**

Say: **You are each building a house with your life—a house that will be tested by failure, personal tragedy, and loneliness. The strength of your life determines the difficulty you can handle. Unfortunately, some people's houses are weak; they need to be strengthened to handle life's problems. Crushed under the weight, some people may choose to have their house disappear—permanently. This destructive choice is called suicide, and it's the topic of our study.**

2. Have You Ever?—(You'll need tape, newsprint, and a marker.) Tape a sheet of newsprint to the wall and divide it in half. Write "Life" on one half and "Death" on the other. Form a circle with kids' arms outstretched and eyes closed. Tell kids to respond appropriately if any of the following statements are true for them. Encourage honesty and openness.

Read these statements, pausing between each one: **Lower your right arm if you've ever felt lonely. Lower your left arm if you've ever not liked yourself. Drop your head if you've ever hurt someone you love. Kneel if you've questioned the purpose and direction of your life. Lie on your back if you've ever been depressed or considered suicide.**

Have kids open their eyes. Then ask: **Why do teenagers attempt or commit suicide?**

Write the answers on the newsprint under "Death." Then have all teenagers lie on their backs with eyes closed. Read these statements, pausing between each one: **Kneel if you've experienced a situation that made you feel good about yourself. Stand with head bowed if you've had someone tell you he or she loves you. Raise your head if you've been praised for something you did well. Raise your left arm if you have a friend.**

Raise your right arm because God loves and accepts you.

Have kids open their eyes. Then ask: **Why do most teenagers choose life over death?**

List these under the "Life" heading on the newsprint. Encourage kids to list more reasons for life than there are reasons listed for death.

Say: **Life is a wonderful gift. The Bible says we're created in God's image and for his purpose. God has a plan for our lives, and he wants us to choose life. Let's look at two men in the Bible whose choices about life had very different outcomes.**

3. If Only—(You'll need paper, Bibles, and pencils.) On separate sheets of paper, write "Peter" and "Judas." Write these scriptures on the appropriate sheet of paper: Peter—Matthew 10:1-8; 14:22-32; Luke 22:54-62; Acts 2:14-41; 4:13-20; 1 Peter 1:1-5; and Judas—Matthew 10:1-8; 26:14-16; 27:3-5; Luke 22:47-48; and Acts 1:12-26.

Form two groups. Give each group paper and a pencil. Have one group read the scriptures about Simon Peter and the other group read about Judas Iscariot. Have groups each write an obituary for their man—but with a twist. Have the groups imagine that instead of Judas committing suicide, Peter did! The Peter group should write an obituary, listing Peter's contributions that wouldn't have occurred because of his premature death. The Judas group should write an obituary, listing the great things God could've done with Judas had he chosen life instead of suicide.

Allow 15 minutes for groups to finish. Then have each group read its obituary.

Ask: **How do you think Peter felt after he denied Jesus? How do you think Judas felt after he betrayed Christ? Was one failure larger than the other? Why or why not? Was suicide Judas' only option? Why or why not? What other options did Judas have?**

Say: **Just as Jesus forgave Peter for his failure, he would've also forgiven Judas. Failure is never final. Jesus can always help us start over if we blow it. People who give up and commit suicide don't give Jesus the opportunity to make their lives stronger and better.**

4. Suicide Solutions—Ask: **Have you known anyone who has attempted or committed suicide? Without using names, explain. How does someone on the verge of suicide feel?**

Say: **There may be someone in your life right now who is deciding whether to choose life or death. That person may even be you. We're going to examine tools for helping friends choose life.**

Call out the following items one at a time: **eyeglasses, telephone, car, pen and paper, money, feet, hands, Bible, and Yellow Pages.** After each object, have kids brainstorm ways to use the object to keep someone from committing suicide. For example, kids may say for the eyeglasses, "Look for ways to encourage depressed friends" or "Seek to learn the warning signs of suicide." Have teenagers add other tools to the list.

Form pairs. Have pairs each role play counseling situations where one partner is considering suicide. Make sure each partner plays the role of counselee and counselor. Remind kids to use the tools they discussed above. (If possible, invite a professional counselor to give tips on what to say to a suicidal friend.)

5. Choose Life—(You'll need three photocopies of the "Choose Life Covenant" on page 98 and a pencil for each person.) Give each person three photocopies of the "Choose Life Covenant."

Say: **One way to save a life is to covenant together to choose life and to be available to people who may be considering suicide.**

Encourage teenagers to covenant with one friend and one adult to choose life by signing each photocopy of the "Choose Life Covenant." Have each person keep a copy of their signed covenant.

6. Closing: "It's A Wonderful Life!"—(You'll need a photocopy of the "It's a Wonderful Life! Card" on page 99 for each person and an ink blotter.) Give each person a photocopy of the "It's a Wonderful Life! Card." After completing the cards, have kids each "sign" their card with a fingerprint, showing their uniqueness and individuality. Have kids each get with their partner from the "Suicide Solutions" activity and read their card. Encourage kids to carry their cards with them.

Close in prayer, thanking God for each person's life and asking for strength for kids to "choose life."

CHOOSE LIFE COVENANT

"Today I ask heaven and earth to be witnesses.
I am offering you life or death,
blessings or curses.
NOW, CHOOSE LIFE!"
(Deuteronomy 30:19)

On this day _____, we
covenant to CHOOSE LIFE in all we do, all we say,
and all we are. As a special creation of God, formed in
his image, each of us is unique and important.

In choosing life, we covenant to

■ share difficulties with each other,

■ encourage each other to choose life if ever
tempted by suicide, and

■ help each other seek out every possible solution,
including professional counseling, if we ever
experience suicidal feelings.

_____
(My signature)

_____
(A friends's signature)

_____
(An adult's signature)

IT'S A WONDERFUL LIFE! CARD

IT'S A WONDERFUL LIFE
(AND I'M SPECIAL)!

I am unique and important because...

I have the special gift or talent of _____

_____.

A thing I love to do is _____

_____.

I have a special relationship with _____

_____.

A dream I have is _____

_____.

One thing I like about me is _____

_____.

Use this Bible study to take kids on a journey to discover what part they play in Christ's body—the church.

OBJECTIVES

In this Bible study kids will

● identify others by telltale body parts,

● experience what it's like to have missing body parts,

● examine the Bible's perspective on Christ's body, and

● identify the part of Christ's body that best fits them.

BEFORE THE BIBLE STUDY

Tack or tape a blanket over an open doorway leaving a foot of open space at the bottom.

Meet in a room with a high ceiling.

Draw a large human body shape on a sheet of newsprint and tape it to the wall. Include major body parts on the drawing such as eyes, ears, mouth, hands, and feet.

Read the Bible study, collect the supplies, and photocopy the handout.

THE BIBLE STUDY

1. Opener: Name That Body Part—(You'll need the blanket tacked or taped over an open doorway.) Welcome kids, then gather by the blanketed doorway. Form two teams. It's okay if the teams are unequal. Tell teams they're going to hold a contest to see who can correctly match the most body parts to their owners. Ask team 1 to go through the doorway on the other side of the blanket. Then, one at a time, have team members each stick their foot, hand, or ear out from underneath the blanket where the other team can see. Have team 2 guess who each body part belongs to. Award 25 points for each correct answer.

Once 10 body parts have been guessed (correctly or incorrectly), have teams switch places and repeat the process. Award points and declare a winning team. (For smaller groups, it's okay for kids to show more than one body part.)

The losing team rewards the winning team by giving them a "hand"—clapping for them.

Say: **We've probably never looked at each other from this unique perspective before. Well, today we're going to take a unique look at Christ's "body parts," and how we as his church fit together.**

2. Missing Parts—(You'll need masking tape and a room with a high ceiling.) Say: **Let's experience how important all body parts are.**

Form teams of four and assign each team member one of these four conditions: You have no right leg; you have no left leg; you have no eyes; you have no hands. (If you have a three-member team, assign only three conditions.)

Give each team a piece of masking tape. While acting out their assignments, have teams each race to see which of them can place the piece of masking tape highest on the wall. Encourage kids to be careful, but try not to assist teams any more than necessary.

After the first round, form teams of kids with the same conditions and have them try it again. For example, combine all kids who have only one leg or combine all kids who have no hands.

After allowing teams several attempts at placing the masking tape higher, congratulate kids for their efforts.

3. What'sa Matta You Body?—Call everyone together and ask: **How did you feel as your team attempted this activity? What did you need to make your job easier? Was it easier or more difficult when your team had the same conditions? Explain. How is your team like being a part of the body of Christ? How is it different? What does this activity tell you about how we should relate to each other in the body of Christ? Is it possible to be a healthy Christian apart from Christ's body? Why or why not?**

Say: **We discovered that the missing body parts affected how well each team accomplished its task. The task was easier when all worked together. Just so, each of us as Christians need one another to be what God has called us to be as his church. There's no such thing as a healthy Christian apart from Christ's body.**

4. This Bod's for You—(You'll need the newsprint with the body shape drawn on it, tape, a Bible and a marker. For each person, you'll need a 3×5 card and a pencil.) Give kids each a 3×5 card and a pencil. Have them each write one way they enjoy serving God or others. When everyone is finished, one at a time, have kids each tape their card to the body part they feel they're most like. For example, a person who'd write, "I like to listen to people's problems," would tape the card on the ear of the body shape. Have kids each explain their card and why they placed it where they did.

Have several volunteers take turns reading aloud 1 Corinthians 12:12-27. Then ask: **What does this passage say about your role in the body of Christ? Why is each part important? What does it say about our role with each other? How can we help and care for each other?**

Write, "The Body of Christ," across the top of the body shape. Point to the body parts where the majority of cards are taped. Ask: **What do you think of the representation of Christ's body here in this room? What are our strengths? What are our weaknesses?**

Point to any blank areas of the newsprint. Ask: **Why are these parts of Christ's body blank? What can we do to fill in the gaps?**

5. Body Work—(You'll need a marker.) Have kids each think of one thing they can do to help fill in the gaps in Christ's body. For example, if there's a gap in the foot area, someone could write that he or she will run an errand for the church office or for a friend this week. Have kids each come up to the body shape and write on the appropriate body part one thing they'll do to help "complete" Christ's body in your youth group. Praise kids for their commitments.

Say: **By seeing ourselves as "one body" rather than focusing on each individual, we can begin to grow in unity and learn to love each other the way Jesus commanded.**

6. Closing: "Body Beautiful" Awards—(You'll need several photocopies of the "Body Beautiful" handout on page 104, scissors, construction paper, glue, and markers. Cut along the dotted lines to separate the pictures.) Have kids arrange themselves in a circle according to their birthdays. In the middle of the circle, set out the award pictures cut from the "Body Beautiful" handout. Give kids each a sheet of construction paper, glue, and a marker. Have kids each create a "Body Beautiful" award for the person on their right. Have kids each choose a picture, glue it to their construction paper, and then write why they chose that picture for the person on their right. For example, "Mandy, I give you this 'Body Beautiful' hand award because you're always willing to lend a helping hand to anyone who asks. Love, Beth."

After all the kids have received their awards, congratulate them on working together to become Christ's beautiful body—the church. Encourage kids to keep their awards as reminders of their vital roles in Christ's body.

Point to the newsprint body shape. Have kids review what they wrote to "complete" the body of Christ. Close with prayer, asking God to give kids strength to fulfill their commitments and become an even more active part of Christ's body in the world.

BODY BEAUTIFUL

"Ear"resistible

Unde"feet"able

"Hand"y to have around

"Eye" admire you

CHAPTER 11

Crowdbreakers and Games

Crowdbreakers and games energize group members and help them "break the ice" at meetings, retreats, lock-ins, or wherever your kids gather. These are the basic requirements of a crowdbreaker or game.

● **It must be first.** Games help kids shut out all the stresses they bring with them to a meeting. Crowdbreakers help kids focus on the learning that'll follow.

● **It must be fun.** Have kids each repeatedly blow up a balloon and release it as they race to get their balloon across a finish line first. Have partners pull off each other's socks—without using their hands. Whatever you do, make it fun!

● **It must be active.** Throw away your paper and pencil activities for crowdbreakers—unless you have kids racing around collecting signatures for the person who can say "Peter Piper picked a peck of pickled peppers" backward or the person with the longest eyelashes. And get kids off their tushes—unless you have them scooting along the floor in an obstacle course or piling on top of each other to build a human totem pole. Crowdbreakers get the adrenalin flowing!

● **It must be creative.** Recycled games are dull. If you always form groups with kids who have matching name tags, you need a creativity booster shot. For tested and true original ideas, check out the crowdbreakers and games in this chapter. Also, get a copy of *Quick Crowdbreakers and Games for Youth Groups* (Group Publishing). You'll be glad you did!

To get an unfamiliar group to interact, here's an idea. Buy envelopes and some bags of jelly beans that have at least nine different colors. In each envelope, insert nine different-color jelly beans.

Give an envelope of jelly beans to each person. Say: **The object of this game is to get nine jelly beans of the same color. Ask others for the color of the jelly bean you want and then trade one of yours. You may trade only one jelly bean at a time.**

This activity takes time because several people may be pursuing jelly beans of the same color. The first person to get nine same-color jelly beans is the winner. Keep playing until everyone has jelly beans of all the same color.

NAME THAT PERSON

Would you expect to find "Clay" working in a pottery shop? or how about "Rose" tending a garden? Give kids each a copy of the "Names!" handout on page 107. Then have individuals or teams compete to see who can come up with the most names in 10 minutes.

Here are the answers.

Name That Girl—1. Melody; 2. Pearl; 3. Dawn; 4. April, May, or June; 5. Candy; 6. Sandy; 7. Pat, Margie, or Marjorene; 8. Lisa or Aleese; 9. Rose, Violet, Lily, or Daisy; 10. Constance; 11. Fanny; 12. Joy, Gladys, Merry, or Mary.

Name That Guy—1. Stew; 2. Jack; 3. Woody, Buzz, or Chip; 4. Nicholas; 5. Clay; 6. Bill; 7. Scott; 8. Chuck; 9. Marlin; 10. Barry or Bud; 11. Frank; 12. Cliff.

NAMES!

Some names just seem to fit who people are or what they do. How many names can you think of that match these descriptions? Write them on the lines following the clues.

Name That Girl...

1. who sings well
_____

2. who lives in an oyster
_____

3. who gets up early
_____

4. who lives on a calendar
_____

5. who's sweet
_____

6. who lives on a beach
_____

7. who lives in a butter dish
_____

8. who rents out apartments
_____

9. who lives in a flowerpot
_____

10. who's always consistent
_____

11. who cools everyone off
_____

12. who's a very happy person
_____

Name That Guy...

1. who's in a pot with carrots and tomatoes _____

2. who lifts a car
_____

3. who lives in a sawmill
_____

4. who gave all his change away _____

5. who makes pottery
_____

6. who's always in the mailbox
_____

7. who lives in a paper-towel rack _____

8. who's tossed into a meat grinder_____

9. who swims in the ocean
_____

10. who grows on bushes
_____

11. who always says what he thinks_____

12. who lives on the edge
_____

OREO SCULPTURES

Group members will have lots-o-fun with this one. Form teams of equal size and give each team several packages of Oreo cookies (or have kids bring their own). Also, give each team two serrated knives, two spoons, a box of toothpicks, and a 4-foot-square piece of posterboard. Say: **Your team has 20 minutes to create a sculpture using the cookies and the tools I've given you. Build your sculpture on the posterboard to help control the mess.**

The white stuff in the Oreos makes great glue or mortar. The brittle part of the cookies can be cut, crushed, or left whole to form creations such as a castle, a Mickey Mouse head, or even a rolling Model T with a garage.

Have everyone vote on the most creative sculpture. Give the winning team a gallon of milk.

PET TALK

Will the real pet owner please stand up? If you'd like your kids to learn more about one another, let their pets do the talking!

Have kids each write on a sheet of paper their name and the name of their pet—or the name they'd give a pet, if they don't have one. Then form teams of three. Collect the papers.

Call the teams—one by one—to stand in front of the others. Announce the names of three pets and have kids guess which pet names belong to which team members. Repeat the process until all teams have finished.

You could award fun pet prizes, such as dog biscuits, to the team whose pet names were easiest to match with the owners.

Your group is sure to discover hilarious pet names and learn new secrets about each other.

POETRY HODGEPODGE

Do you have a Shakespeare somewhere in your group? Here's a quick way to find out. Form small groups. Give each group an envelope containing a nonrhyming poem that has been cut into two-line pieces. Each envelope should have the same poem in it.

Ask groups to reconstruct their poems as they think the author wrote it. Then have a person from each group read the revamped poem. The more variations, the better. After each group has shared its creative labor, read the true version of the poem.

This crowdbreaker also works at holiday parties when you use poems that reflect the occasion.

POSTCARD PASTE-UP

Use this fun crowdbreaker before a meeting about God's creation or the Apostle Paul's missionary journeys.

Collect about 40 picture postcards of scenery. Cut each in half. Place a card table with one half of each postcard, a stapler, and a few pencils in the center of the room. Place an empty wastebasket beside the table.

Hide the other halves of the postcards all over the room and anywhere else you want your kids to go.

On "go," have kids race to find the hidden postcard halves. When a group member finds a hidden half, he or she must run back to the table, staple it together with the other half, sign it, and "mail" it in the wastebasket.

When all the cards are mailed in the wastebasket, count the signatures to discover who found the most. Give that person an appropriate grand prize such as a book of postage stamps.

TALKING SENSES

If you want the kids in your youth group to learn more about each other, let their senses do the talking!

Form groups of two or three. Have kids each choose one of their senses—sight, touch, smell, taste, or hearing—and tell about a great memory that's tied to that sense.

Kids might talk about the smell of baked beans and how that reminds them of Grandma's house. Or maybe the mountains remind them of a life-changing retreat. Encourage kids to explain why their memories are important.

After all group members have talked about one "sense memory," have each group report to everyone else in the room. Have each person talk about one memory of someone in his or her small group. Then have group members lock arms in a circle and thank God for the "sensory" experiences they just had.

WILEY WARM-UPS

Sometimes kids need to "warm up" before they begin an activity. Use these ideas to lead everyone into action.

● **Nose Song**—Have kids find a partner and sing "Row, Row, Row Your Boat" in unison while they hold their partner's nose.

● **Backward Writing**—Challenge kids each to write their name and address backward. Applaud the first person to finish with no errors.

● **Cracker Mouth**—Have kids each pick up a saltine cracker off a table with their mouth (no hands allowed). Tell them to eat it and then whistle, "New York, New York."

● **Paddy Cake Relay**—Form two teams for a relay race. The first person in each line runs to a designated point, touches it, returns to the line, and plays "paddy cake" with the next person in line. This process continues until one of the teams finishes (and wins).

Community Builders

Community-builders are a vital part of any youth ministry. Why? Because they provide the avenue for kids to get to know each other (and other church members) more deeply—to share their struggles and victories.

When planning your own community-builders, consider these foundational tips.

● **Make it inclusive.** Don't plan an active community-builder when you know you'll have disabled kids in your group who won't be able to participate fully. Find ways to creatively include all your kids in the experience.

● **Leave it open to newcomers.** Design your community-builders so that even if new people come to your group, they'll feel welcome. Don't create an "unspoken" rule that sharing times must be deeply personal. If you ask kids what good thing happened to them this week, accept both "deep" and "superficial" answers equally.

● **Don't underestimate the importance of building community.** Jesus spent a great deal of his time doing nothing but building community among his disciples. So should you. Recognize that kids are looking for a place to belong first—and *then* a place to learn and grow. If you help provide them with their first priority, they'll be more willing and ready to focus on growing in their faith.

Don't be afraid to dedicate a whole meeting—even a series of meetings—to nothing other than building community. The benefits of laying a good foundation now will pay off in the long run.

ALL-CHURCH VIDEO

Here's a great way to promote intergenerational togetherness. Have your youth group videotape various church events throughout the year.

Decide which events they'll tape and who'll be in charge of covering specific events. For example, have one group member cover a Wednesday-night administrative meeting and have another capture a Sunday school program. Ask kids to be on constant lookout for human interest shots, such as a dad holding his son or a young person helping an elderly lady to her seat. Urge kids to mix comedy with drama, to have planned scenes mixed with candid shots, and to highlight as many people as possible.

Have kids edit the videotapes and dub in music. Then schedule an all-church dinner-and-movie affair.

CANDLE WITH CARE

This activity works best on an overnight activity when most of your group members are present.

Give each group member an unlighted candle, such as a 6-inch taper. Have kids sit in a circle around a large candle. Turn off all lights, and light the large candle.

Talk about how the qualities of the large candle represent the qualities of group members; for example, its brightness, independence, beauty, power, and warmth. Then point out how the candle's limitations are similar to group members' limitations; for example, only one light with so much darkness around it.

Tell what the youth group means to you and how it has changed you. Then light your candle from the large candle. Have group members who've brought visitors each light their guests' candle. Ask group members to each tell what the youth group means to them and how God has used it to change them. After kids have each answered the question, have them light their candle from the large candle.

When every candle is lit, the light will illumine the room. Read

112

aloud John 8:12. Explain how one youth group can make a big difference in a dark world.

Have kids blow out their candles one at a time, leaving the center candle burning. Close with prayer, thanking God for each person in the youth group and the difference the group can make in the world.

CREATE A GREAT DATE

Are your kids stumped for ideas for inexpensive fun dates? Then try this.

For two or three weeks, have your group collect creative ideas for dates. Some might collect newspaper advertisements for local plays, pamphlets about zoos or museums, or coupons for free hot dogs. Or have kids write ideas on slips of paper such as ice skating, visiting the airport, going on a wintertime picnic, or hanging out at the bookstore. Have kids bring their ideas to youth group meetings and place them in a hat.

After you've collected an abundance of ideas, at a youth meeting have kids draw ideas out of the hat and read them aloud. Have a volunteer write the ideas on newsprint.

Form small groups. Have each group create a great date using the ideas listed on the newsprint and any new ideas they might have. Each group's date must be inexpensive and active. The entire date must be planned to include transportation, activities, and food. After five minutes, have each group tell about its great date. Award tickets to a petting zoo or school play to the group with the most creative date.

FOOTPRINTS

Here's how your kids can "leave their mark" on the group. Paint one of the walls white in your youth room and hang a copy of the *Footprints* poem in the middle of it (the poem is available at most Christian bookstores). In a short ceremony-fashion, read aloud 1 Corinthians 12:12-27 and the *Footprints* poem. Talk about how important each person is to the body and how God always cares for us.

Then have each person in the group put a footprint on the wall. You can do this by painting kids' feet using several different colors, and then have them each "stamp" their mark on the wall. Footprints can be placed high on the wall by stacking chairs. On their footprint, have kids each use a black marker to write their name and high school graduation date.

LIP SERVICE

Are you interested in building a bridge between the adult church members and the teenagers in your congregation? If so, Lip Service is a way to connect those two groups.

The Lip Service program allows adults to support and encourage your young people through prayer. Adults who want to be involved each make a three-month commitment to pray daily for a teenager. Participating adults can remind their teenagers that they're praying for them by calling them or sending cards.

After three months, adults are asked about future involvement. Those who wish to continue Lip Service are assigned a different teenager for the next three months.

A great variation on this community-builder is to simply turn the tables! Assign volunteer young people to specific adults in your congregation and have them pray daily for one-month time periods. Encourage kids to send cards of support during the month that they're praying.

NEWLYWED GAME

We all know the benefits of occasional parent-teen meetings. But we don't always have an easy time planning the programming. Here's a fun idea that works well.

Before the meeting, ask parents and teenagers to dress like parents dressed when the parents were first married.

Then, for an activity guaranteed to be hilarious, try a different version of The Newlywed Game. Ask for volunteers to be the game-show host and his lovely assistant. Then have four "couples" portray newlyweds. The couples can be either parents or teenagers, or mixtures of both. They should not be real-life married couples.

Send the four "husbands" to another room while the host asks the four "wives" each questions about their marriage. Questions might be about where they met, what the husband likes for breakfast, or how the wife curls her hair. Have the assistant write their answers on newsprint. Then have the husbands come back in. Ask the husbands the same four questions and compare the responses. Award special treats to the couple with the most matching answers.

For refreshments, serve fondue or another favorite from parents' newlywed days.

WHERE ARE YOUR LEADERS?

This is a great way to help kids get to know their adult leaders and volunteers!

Form as many teams as you have adult leaders. Give each team a set of clues—serious and silly—each regarding the identity of a different leader. For example, "This person was caught painting the high school lawn red, has brown hair, is an accomplished puzzle-builder, craves pistachio nuts, and reads comic books in bed."

Have the leaders each stay in their homes with prepared refreshments and personal momentos such as scrapbooks, trophies, or handmade crafts. Instruct teams to each read their set of clues and go to the house of the person who fits those clues. If the guess is wrong, the team must try again. If the team guesses correctly, the team members may stay at that house, enjoy the refreshments, and learn more about that leader by asking questions about his or her occupation and interests.

After one hour, have teams and leaders gather at your house for games and more food. Use crowdbreakers and games that'll help kids and leaders get to know each other better.

YOUTH DICTIONARY

Think of the slang or faddish words your group members use. How many of those words do you know the meaning of? Open the lines of communication by compiling a Youth Dictionary with your group members.

Have group members write their slang words. Then form the list to look like a dictionary by putting the words in alphabetical order and showing how to pronounce each one. Tell what part of speech each word is such as a noun or an adjective, and have young people give their definition.

The group will fill several pages in no time. Have volunteers type the Youth Dictionary, photocopy it, and arrange it in booklet form. Distribute copies to parents and other church members. Adults may not change their vocabulary, but they'll understand kids' language better. Update the dictionary as needed. Use it as a discussion starter on understanding others.

YOUTH GROUP PRAYER PROJECT

Help your kids put prayer into practice with this community-builder.

Obtain a set of mailing labels preprinted with the names and addresses of church members. Then photocopy a short form letter for each family or person on the mailing list, telling people they'll be prayed for by the youth group kids during the coming week. Also photocopy some practical prayer suggestions for kids to use.

During a youth group meeting, give each person two or three mailing labels, envelopes, and form letters. Or give out some names each week for a few weeks. Also supply stamps and the prayer suggestions.

Have kids mail their letters, and then pray daily for the people they mailed them to.

At a later meeting, have church members tell kids ways their prayers were answered during the time kids were praying.

Devotions

U sing quick devotions is a great way to crystalize a learning experience for kids on the spot. In fact, a devotion's strength rests in its versatility and timeliness. A devotion about controlling the tongue at the end of a 12-hour lock-in may have much more effect than an entire study on tongue-taming in another setting.

The other strength devotions possess is their compact nature. Most devotions last no more than 10 minutes. That's good news for youth groups on the go. And who knows? Those 10 minutes could change a life.

Well-designed devotions should contain seven essential elements. You'll find these elements in each of the devotions included in this chapter. Use this same approach when designing your own devotions for your ministry.

● **Theme**—This is the topic of the devotion. It should be simple and concise.

● **Scripture**—The passage should be relatively short, and it should directly apply to the theme.

● **Overview**—Distill the devotion's main point down into one sentence. This will help you crystalize it in your mind.

● **Preparation**—List all the items you might need for the devotion. Keep the list simple and be sure you have all the preparation done long before the devotion begins.

● **Experience**—This is the "meat" of the devotion—the unique element that lets kids actually experience the theme. Kids use all their physical senses to gain a deeper understanding of the topic discussed.

● **Response**—Participants take the experience one step further by thinking about what they've experienced and how it applies to their lives.

● **Closing**—Each devotion should conclude with a prayer or activity that summarizes the devotional thought and helps kids apply it to their lives.

A NEW YEAR, A NEW YOU

Topic—New Year's

Scripture—2 Corinthians 5:17-19

Overview—Kids will see how something old and worthless can become new and worthwhile.

Preparation—Collect things out of the garbage such as empty cans, cardboard boxes, egg cartons, and plastic containers. You'll also need tempera paint, paint brushes, glue, construction paper, scissors, markers, and a Bible.

Experience—Give each person a piece of garbage. Say: **The previous owner of your object thought it was old and worthless. Make something new out of it using the art supplies.**

Response—After everyone has finished, ask: **How did you feel when I first gave you a piece of trash? Now what do you think of your piece of trash? What can you learn from this experience?**

Say: **When the new year starts, we often look at the bad things in our lives and resolve to improve them. Think about one of the things you want to improve.**

Have a volunteer read aloud 2 Corinthians 5:17-19. Then say: **Just as you transformed this piece of trash, Jesus can help you transform bad habits into good ones. You can become a new creation with Christ's help. You can become a new you for the new year.**

Ask: **How does this passage challenge you as you look at a new year? How does it comfort you?**

Closing—Have group members sit in a circle and set their new creations in front of them. Then close with prayer, thanking God for the power to change as Christians.

Topic—Sin and forgiveness

Scripture—Romans 3:23; 2 Corinthians 5:21; and 1 John 1:9

Overview—Kids will experience the effects of sin and the power of God's forgiveness.

Preparation—You'll need newspaper, a Bible, and a damp white towel.

Experience—Give group members each a sheet of newspaper. Tell them they hold "sin" in their hands. Have them each wad their sin into a tiny ball. Then read aloud Romans 3:23.

Afterward, have kids each drop their sin and look at their hands. Ask: **How do you feel as you look at your sin-stained hands? How is the ink on your hands like or unlike sin's real effects on us? Explain.**

Response—Read aloud 1 John 1:9. Say: **This towel is Jesus. As Jesus comes to you, wipe sin's effects on Jesus—remembering he died to take away your sins.**

Ask kids to remain silent during this activity. Pass the damp white towel to all group members and have them each wipe their hands clean.

Closing—Hold up the towel so everyone can see the dark smudges on it. Read aloud 2 Corinthians 5:21. Ask: **If Jesus became sin, is he still sinful?**

Then pray: **Thank you, Jesus, for dying for our sins. Thank you for loving us and forgiving us. In Jesus' name, amen.**

Topic—Perseverance

Scripture—Romans 5:3-5

Overview—Kids will practice patience and perseverance by trying to thread a needle.

Preparation—You'll need a needle with a tiny eye and a 12-inch-long thread for each person. You'll also need a Bible, a pincushion, and Con-Tact paper.

Experience—Give kids each a needle and thread. Have them try to thread their needles in 30 seconds.

Afterward, ask: **How did you feel as you tried to thread your needle? How did you feel when you succeeded? when you failed? Why were some people more successful than others?**

Talk about how people who persevere or who have had more practice at something are usually more successful than people who give up.

Response—Read aloud Romans 5:3-5. Have kids gather around a table with a pincushion on it. Tell kids to each think of an area they need perseverance in. Then have them each keep their thread and one at a time stick their needles in the pincushion as they say to themselves, "I commit to stick it out when I feel like giving up in _____."

Closing—Give kids each a square-inch piece of Con-Tact paper. Have them each place their thread on the sticky side of the Con-Tact paper and fold the paper over. Have them keep their thread and paper as a reminder to persevere when they feel like giving up.

SLOW DOWN

Topic—Rest

Scripture—John 4:4-6

Overview—Kids will experience what it's like not to rest and decide how they'll take time to rest this week.

Preparation—You'll need a Bible. You'll also need a sheet of paper and a pencil for each person.

Experience—Lead the group in five minutes of nonstop calisthenics. Don't let anyone rest. Shout out exercises such as jog in place as fast as you can, do 25 sit-ups, do 15 push-ups, do 30 jumping jacks, and jog around the room backward twice. Continue shouting out different strenuous exercises until the five minutes are up and kids are obviously tired.

Response—As group members rest, ask: **How did it feel to do**

strenuous exercise without stopping? What would've happened if you had exercised for one hour straight? Why is rest important?

Have a volunteer read aloud John 4:4-6. Then ask: What did Jesus do in this passage? Explain. How important is rest? Why is it tempting not to rest? How often do you rest? How do you rest and relax?

Closing—Give kids each a sheet of paper and a pencil. Have them each write one way they resolve to make time to rest this week.

Form groups of three. Have kids each tell their group members how they plan to make time to rest this week. Then have the groups close in prayer, asking for God's help to rest and relax.

Outreach and Service Projects

Y our youth group is like an old shoe. Comfortable. Kids are satisfied with the status quo. They enjoy having fun and seeing their friends at the meetings. They like throwing parties.

But then you launch your group into a service project. And things begin to happen.

Kids gain confidence. They boost others' self-esteem. Their faith grows. And they develop lasting relationships with those less fortunate than they are.

Use these ideas (and your own!) to help kids take those scary but healthy steps toward Christian maturity. The needs are all around you. But the need is also in your group—the need to serve others and show themselves to be growing toward Christ.

As you do your service and outreach projects, remember these tips.

● **Harbor no hidden agendas.** When serving others, they're always suspicious of your hidden motives. Do you expect them to come to your church in exchange for this service? Do you expect them to let you talk to them about Jesus in exchange for this service? If you do have an expectation, lay it on the table. People resent being tricked or feeling manipulated.

● **Do excellent work.** Stress to kids that serving others isn't a matter of "you get what you pay for." It's a way to demonstrate the perfect love of God. So make your work shine!

● **Make it fun.** Don't make the mistake of teaching kids that serving others is a dull chore that we have to do because we're Christians. It's fun! Help kids see the fun in serving by mixing fun games into the projects. The examples in this chapter offer great ideas of ways to make serving others a blast!

BLOOD LINES

Take kids on an outing to donate a pint of blood at a local clinic or hospital. Or better yet, have your youth group join with a hospital and a Christian school organization to launch a blood drive on your school campus. Include lunch-time workshops on AIDS and its impact on the nation's blood supply.

CREATIVE CONCERN

Use your group's creativity to remember less-fortunate people.

Divide the group into teams and give each team a large box. Each team has one hour to fill the box with clothes, food, toys, and other gifts. Encourage kids to think about what the recipients might like to have.

After everyone has returned to the meeting place, award prizes for creativity in selecting items and practicality of the items themselves. Then have a meeting on ministering to the needs in your community.

Have teenagers volunteer to take the boxes to a children's home, orphanage, denominational relief agency, or other social service organization.

INSTANT REPLAY

Here's an easy-to-coordinate outreach to players and coaches.

Set up viewing equipment in a large room in your church. Then videotape a local school's football game.

Invite the team and coaches, along with your young people, to view the game video immediately after the game. Serve hamburgers, hot dogs, or chili. Ask local merchants to donate soft drinks, ice, chips, or dessert.

SHELTER GIVE-AWAY

Have kids pick up gift certificates for sporting events, skating rinks, pizza restaurants, amusement parks, or the local recreation center. Then have kids take them to the nearest homeless shelter and give them to homeless parents with small children.

SHOPPING CART SCAVENGER HUNT

Send your kids on the most unforgettable shopping trip they've ever been on. And help the needy in your area at the same time.

Contact a local food bank ahead of time to learn what items it needs most. Then make a "grocery list" of 15 or 20 of the items. Get permission to borrow shopping carts from a local grocery store.

Form teams of no more than four. Give each team a shopping cart and a grocery list. Have teams go door-to-door in search of the items on the list. Award a pizza to the first team to return with its shopping completed.

When everyone is back, have a discussion about giving. Use Deuteronomy 15:7-10; Proverbs 25:21; Matthew 10:42; 22:34-40; Acts 20:35; Romans 12:6-13; and 2 Corinthians 9:6-9 as discussion starters.

Then go together to take the food kids collected to the food bank.

SHOPPING IN THE FAST LANE

Even the hyperbusy kids in your group can take time out to serve others. When kids go on their normal grocery store rounds, ask them to buy extra cans of soup, stew, fruit, or vegetables for a hungry family in your area. Then have them drop the food in a donation box at your church or group meeting room.

Have group members take turns delivering weekly donations to your local food bank during lunch breaks.

UNDERGROUND OUTREACH

Help kids break the ice when they want to talk about the Lord. Have group members ask their friends at school the "Questions For Your Friends" on page 126. Then publish the results, along with group members' comments, in an "underground" youth group paper. Use clip art to spice up the paper. You'll have an eager audience because teenagers love to see their opinions in print.

WINDOW WASHING

Let the sunshine in with this outreach project. Kids will get to know each other and provide a service to their community.

About four weeks before your work date, canvas several neighborhoods in your area to see who would be interested in having the windows washed on the outside of their houses—free of charge. Explain that it's a community service provided by your church's youth group as a practical way to show people God's love.

Form groups of four. Have each group provide two buckets, a large sponge, a squeegee, a small ladder, a water hose, a bottle of dish-washing liquid, and rags.

Divide your appointments into work assignments. Each group can do, six to eight houses in one day.

Have kids wipe windows with slightly soapy water, rinse with clear water, and squeegee the water off.

QUESTIONS FOR YOUR FRIENDS

Ask your friends the following questions and record their answers.

1. Who is Jesus Christ?

2. Do you believe Jesus rose from the dead? Why or why not?

3. Do you believe Jesus is the only way to God? Why or why not?

4. What makes someone a Christian?

5. In John 3:3 Jesus says we must be born again to have eternal life. How do you become born again?

6. Do you feel it's important to have a personal relationship with Jesus Christ? Why or why not?

7. If you could ask God a question, what would it be?

CHAPTER 15

Fund-Raisers

Are fund-raisers right for your youth group? Although most youth groups probably use fund-raisers, the debate continues on the "rightness" of raising money for ministry outside the church.

As you consider fund raising as a part of your youth ministry, check out these pros and cons.

Pros:

● Fund raising promotes evangelism by getting kids out into the community.

● Fund raising offers loads of leadership opportunities for kids.

● Fund raising gives churched and nonchurched people alike a chance to affirm your ministry.

● Fund raising builds a strong sense of community in your youth group.

Cons:

● Fund raising isn't a part of biblical stewardship principles.

● Fund raising devalues youth ministry in the church by forcing young people to go outside the church for support—unlike any other ministry in the church.

● Fund raising takes away valuable time from kids when they could be ministering without being concerned about money.

● Fund raising might eventually endanger the church's status as "nonprofit," because fund-raisers often involve selling a product or service for a profit.

There you have it. The rest is up to you.

Even if you decide fund raising isn't a good idea for your particular group, the ideas in this chapter can still be used. Just take out the dollar signs, and *voilà!* You've got a great bundle of fun events for your youth ministry!

AUCTION-A-MENU

Here's a tasty way to raise money for your youth group and promote fellowship within the church.

Ask for volunteers from your church who are willing to open their homes, and prepare and serve meals for four people. Have cooks each submit a menu of the meal they'll serve and the date they'll serve it. The date should be within a couple of weeks.

Then auction off the menus following a church service or event. Withhold the names of those preparing the meals to allow interaction between people who don't ordinarily get together.

The auction can be done two ways. Either four individuals can bid on each menu, or one person can bid on each menu and bring three guests.

Bon appétit!

BETHLEHEM REVISITED

Expect lots of people from your church and community to come to this unforgettable fund-raiser. The object is to re-create the street scene in Bethlehem 2,000 years ago—the sights, sounds, and smells. It all takes place within the rooms of your own church.

Have youth group members dress in costumes as carpenters, tent-makers, food-sellers, basket-makers, animal-traders, Roman soldiers, rude and polite innkeepers, children musicians, lepers, and beggars. Decorate the rooms and the "street" to look as antique as possible. Make the scene realistic—live animals such as doves, huge plants, a carpenter tapping rhythmically while a potter's wheel drones, a rabbi teaching his students, women baking bread. Be creative!

When visitors come in, census-takers can have them sign their names on a scroll. Beggars who roam the street can gladly take donations (this is your income). Amidst the hubbub, there's talk of a Messiah coming to save the world. The tour might last 20 or 30 minutes. Finally, at the end of the street in a quiet, out-of-the-way spot, sightseers enter a dimly lit stable where shepherds and a young couple are rejoicing. Mary, the handmaid of the Lord, has brought forth a son and laid him in a manger.

It's the next best thing to being in Bethlehem!

CELEBRITY TREASURE HUNT

Here's an exciting way to collect funds for the group's next trip or mission project.

Enlist the support of a local celebrity (sports personality, TV weatherperson, political figure) in advance. The celebrity is the "treasure" everyone will seek.

A few days before the treasure hunt, divide the group into teams. Tell teams that the day of the hunt they'll each get a free set of general clues that you've composed. Solving the first clue leads to the location of the second clue, and so on until the treasure is found. For example, the first clue could say, "Place-kicker's delight, turn to the right." The team would then look for the second clue, which is taped to the goal post in the football field down the street to the right. This clue would then lead the team to the third clue, and so on.

Now for the money-making twist—since the object is to find the treasure first, teams will want extra clues that offer more specific directions. To obtain these extra clues, team members must solicit sponsors who will buy the clues for them. Charge a set fee for each clue. The number of clues teams can buy is unlimited. For example, to help find the clue taped to the goal post, an extra clue could be bought that says, "Think 'goal posts'!"

Station the celebrity at a specific location just before the hunt starts. Each member of the team that finds the celebrity first receives an autographed picture of the celebrity or some other incentive.

CLOWN-O-GRAM SURPRISES

Use the clowns in your group to deliver unexpected messages of love. Publicize your service in the usual ways—church newsletter, posters, fliers, word of mouth. Dress up as clowns during announcement time at church. Let people know that the purpose of a clown-o-gram is to make people happy! You can deliver clown-o-grams to friends, relatives, spouses, children, and elderly people. Special occasions such as birthdays and anniversaries also offer opportunities.

Duplicate several 3×5 cards to give to senders. Each card should have a space for the sender's name, address, and phone number. The bottom of the card should include options the sender has for what he or she wants you to deliver, such as a song, a poem, balloons, a card, or flowers.

Charge a fee for clown-o-grams. Call the recipients the day before your delivery to confirm their availability. Then gather a team of clowns, dress up, and start clowning around!

FLOAT-IN THEATER

What happens when you combine a swimming pool, movie, and freewill offering? Money waterlogs your youth fund!

Splash your church with publicity for a floating "drive-in" theater. On movie night, place the projector and screen at pool side near the shallow end so the nonswimmers will feel comfortable alongside the more fishy types. Rent or distribute inflated rafts and inner tubes to people for comfort while they float. Sell refreshments (keep them out of the pool) and provide plenty of trash bags for a quick cleanup. Assign lifeguards to ensure the safety of the audience.

Schedule two or more performances. At the end of each show, explain the purpose of your fund-raiser, take a freewill offering and watch the money rain down.

Special reminder—before you rent the film, confirm with the film producer that it's legal for you to publicize and show the film in front of a group for fund-raising purposes. Also explain that you won't be charging an admission fee but will take a freewill offering at the end of the show.

LUMBERJACK BREAKFAST

Breakfast at night? If Denny's can do it, so can your group!

Publicize a nighttime lumberjack breakfast and sell tickets a few weeks ahead of time. Charge about $3 for adults and $1.50 for 5- to 12-year-olds. Children under 5 eat free. Ask people to dress like lumberjacks in flannel shirts, overalls, and work boots.

On the day of the breakfast, have kids decorate the dining area to look like an old log cabin. Use checkered tablecloths, kerosene lamps, and old axes and saws.

Then welcome the congregation to a nighttime breakfast bonanza of pancakes, eggs, sausage, bacon, ham, grits, biscuits, gravy, juice, and coffee. Have kids dressed like "bunkhouse cooks" do the cooking and serving.

After the breakfast, have an old-time sing-along. Use fun songs everyone will know. Then give special recognition for the most authentically dressed family.

MONEY WALL

This one's sure to be an attention-grabber and a fun project. First, have group members create a lively poster describing the fund-raiser's purpose and how the money will be spent. Next, pick a relatively blank wall in your church building. Tape the poster onto the center of the wall. Then announce to the congregation your plans to wallpaper the wall—with money.

Encourage people to read the poster and tape their dollars onto the wall. Have contributors start taping money on one corner of the wall with the goal of covering the whole wall. Set out rolls of tape nearby.

When the leaves pile up this fall, serve your community and pile up a few greenbacks. Determine how many yards your group wants to rake and then have group members secure pledges from sponsors. Suggest a minimum of 15 cents for each yard raked.

Ask everyone to bring a rake and meet at the church on a scheduled Saturday morning. A group of eight can rake about 30 yards in one day.

Choose a nearby neighborhood with lots of dead leaves and explain to the homeowners that you're offering a free raking service. After raking each yard, have the homeowner sign a sheet to show you completed the job. You might even leave a brochure describing your church.

Retreats

"Why do we have retreats?" is a question that's well worth your time. Worthy goals for a retreat include fun, fellowship, recreation, Bible study, issues study, discipleship, and faith growth. Any one retreat may include several of these goals or others you find important.

A general purpose statement for all retreats could be, "To set apart a time from the ordinary events of life when a specific group of people can relate to each other through a variety of modes centered around a common theme." Well in advance of retreat, meet with your steering committee to develop a purpose statement. Then brainstorm with leaders to list specific goals such as

- to build closer relationships,
- to develop better understandings of God's Word,
- to study issues faced by kids today, and
- to study a current social issue facing our world.

Work with your steering committee to create a retreat plan that follows the general purpose statement and meets the specific goals you've all agreed on.

Use the following retreat outlines as examples for how your retreat outlines should look when they're finished. And remember, whatever the purpose of your retreat, make sure it has lots of opportunity for fun. That's one of the main reasons kids like to go!

Looking for Truth in All the Right Places

Jesus says our goal in life is to love God with all we are. But the world says we should seek pleasure. Who's telling the truth?

Clearly, teenagers have no easy task in discovering God's truth in a darkened world. What's the answer?

Turn on the light! There's no better place to find truth than in scripture. This retreat pits God's truth against the world's lies. These Bible-based experiences will help your group members understand their confusing world and choose a path that will bring them closer to God and one another.

OBJECTIVES

In this retreat kids will
- identify ways society distorts truth,
- discover the truths Jesus proclaims about himself,
- role play scenes of deceit from the Bible,
- design skits that satirize advertising claims,
- develop closer friendships with one another, and
- celebrate God's good news through creative worship.

RETREAT PREPARATION

- **Lie Busters**—Write on separate slips of paper the scripture reference Ephesians 4:25 and each participant's name. Put the paper slips in an envelope marked "Lie Busters."
- **Truth-or-Lie? Games**—On separate sheets of paper, draw a house, triangle, circle, square, and happy face.
- Collect supplies and photocopy handouts.

RETREAT SCHEDULE

Friday

5 p.m.	Covenant for Growth and Lie Busters
7:45 p.m.	Arrival and Setup
8:15 p.m.	Welcome and Announcements
8:30 p.m.	Truth-or-Lie? Games

9:30 p.m. Deceiver's Theater
10:30 p.m. Snacks
11 p.m.   Cut It Out!
11:30 p.m. Pack It in for the Night

Saturday

7:15 a.m. Rise and Shine
7:45 a.m. Blank-Face Place Mats
8 a.m.   Friendship Walk #1
8:30 a.m. Breakfast
9:15 a.m. True Calisthenics
9:30 a.m. Captured Sheep Bible Study
10:45 a.m. Break
11 a.m.   VISA Card Blues
Noon   Lunch
1:15 p.m. Friendship Walk #2
1:45 p.m. Free Time
5 p.m.   "They Want Me to What?" Skit Planning
6:15 p.m. Supper
7:30 p.m. "They Want Me to What?" Skits
9 p.m.   Journey of Light
10 p.m.   Not-Ready-for-Prime-Time Video Event
11 p.m.   Light of the World Evensong
11:30 p.m. Pack It in for the Night

Sunday

7:15 a.m. Rise and Shine
8 a.m.   Friendship Walk #3
8:30 a.m. Breakfast
9:15 a.m. True Calisthenics
9:30 a.m. True Worship Preparation
10 a.m.   True Worship
11 a.m.   Pack and Depart

THE RETREAT

Friday
● **Covenant for Growth Opener**—Before you leave for the
retreat, give kids each a photocopy of the "Covenant for Growth"

135

handout on page 137. Ask them to each read and sign it.

● **Lie Busters**—You'll need the "Lie Busters" envelope and a Bible. On the way to the retreat, or before you leave if you're not all riding together, read aloud Ephesians 4:25.

Say: **On this retreat, we'll learn more about the difference between truth and lies. As a way of reminding one another about the truths God tells us, each one of us will be a "Lie Buster" for one other person. At least once each day, secretly leave a short, affirming note for your "secret friend," reminding him or her about one of God's truths. Don't tell anyone who your secret friend is.**

Give kids each a slip of paper from your "Lie Busters" envelope. Make sure no one receives his or her own name.

● **Truth-or-Lie? Games**—Say: **To start things off, let's play three games that'll reveal how easy it is to distort the truth.**

● **Pass the Phrase**—Sit in a circle. Give participants each a 3×5 card and a pencil. On your 3×5 card, write, "The grass is tall and green; the sky is sunny and blue; the night is dark and scary."

Say: **The goal of this game is to write—accurately—the phrase your neighbor will show you. You'll have just three seconds to read what's written on your neighbor's 3×5 card. Then write that message on your card. I'll start by showing the phrase to my neighbor. Then each person will do the same until the phrase comes back to me.**

Have kids count aloud, "1,001; 1,002; 1,003," as each person shows the phrase to his or her neighbor. After the phrase has gone all the way around the circle, compare the original message to the end product.

Then ask: **Why was the end message different from the actual message? Have you ever told someone something, and then found that your message got distorted along the way? Explain. How do you feel when someone spreads something untrue about you?**

● **Back Drawing**—You'll need the drawings of a house, triangle, circle, square, and happy face. Form teams of no more than five. Have kids in each team sit one behind the other in single file. Give a sheet of paper and a marker to the front person in each team. Ask the last person in each team to come up to the front.

136

Covenant for Growth

I, _____,
hereby covenant with the other
group members on this retreat
to be enthusiastic, caring and
supportive. I agree to follow
retreat guidelines and actively
participate in all activities. I will
pray and seek God's direction
during this special time.

Signed

_____

Pick one of the objects you drew and show it to each person. Then have them each go back to their group, and use their finger to draw the object on the back of the person in front of them.

Then have the next person in line (the one whose back was just used as a drawing surface) draw the object on the back of the next person. That person should draw the object based on the sensations he or she felt as the object was drawn on his or her back.

Continue to the front of each line, and then have the first person in each line draw on paper what was drawn on his or her back.

Have kids compare their team's drawing to the original.

Then ask: **How did it feel to draw an object based on so little information? Can you think of something that's happened to you that was similar to this exercise? Explain.**

● **All or Nothing**—Form a circle. Have kids think of three personal facts. All must be true, or all must be false. For example, a person might say, "I broke my arm when I was 4. I learned to water-ski when I was 10. I have visited the Grand Canyon."

Have kids take turns telling their facts. After each set of facts, have kids vote on whether the facts are true or false. Kids win one M&M's candy for each person they fooled. The person with the most M&M's at the end of the game wins the rest of the bag.

Ask: **Was it easy or hard for you to think up lies about yourself? To get others to believe your lies? For someone to fool you with a lie? Explain.**

● **Deceiver's Theater**—Scatter the following props on the floor—bathrobes, a burlap bag or carpet remnant, wigs, sandals, pots and pans, silverware, a pillow, and a sleeping bag or bed linen. You'll need a Bible. Say: **In the Old Testament we find a very powerful story about deceit. Tonight we'll act out that story.**

Ask a few volunteers to read aloud the story of Jacob and Esau in Genesis 25:19-34; 27:1-45. Then ask for four volunteers to play the roles of Jacob, Esau, Rebekah, and Isaac.

Say: **These four volunteers will start acting out the story of Jacob and Esau, but at any point in the drama—even in midsentence—a character may tag someone else to step in and continue the role. The other actors must freeze until the tagged person assumes his or her role. Use as many of the** props on the floor as you can. We'll keep going until the story's completed.

Encourage kids to tag others often during the drama.

After the drama, ask: **What would you have done if you'd been Jacob? Esau? Rebekah? Isaac? Who's the worst character in this story? Who's the best? Are most people liars? When has a lie cost you dearly? Is there anyone you can trust to not lie? Has God ever lied to you?**

Say: **Everything we've experienced shows us it's easy to lie or be lied to. Sometimes it's hard to tell the difference between a truth and a lie. Fortunately, God can help us.**

● **Cut It Out!**—You'll need a ball of yarn, a Bible, and a pair of scissors. Form a circle.

Say: **This ball of yarn represents different lies we've heard today. Think of one lie the world tried to tell you today. For example, you might have seen a billboard on the way here that implied that alcohol is the key to having a good time.**

Ask a volunteer to tell about a lie he or she heard during the day. Give that person the ball of yarn, and ask him or her to hang on to the end of the yarn and throw the ball to someone else. Have that person tell about a lie, hang on to a section of yarn, and then throw the ball to someone else. Continue until everyone has had a turn and the yarn has woven the kids together.

Say: **Lies can bind us up, but God's truth brings freedom.**

Have a volunteer read aloud John 8:31-47. Pass a pair of scissors around the circle and have kids cut the yarn.

Say: **Jesus says if we listen and receive his word, his truth will set us free. Think of one lie that's binding you up that you'd like Jesus to cut away. As we close in prayer, feel free to ask God aloud to set you free from that lie.**

Close with a prayer thanking God for his truth.

Saturday

● **Blank-Face Place Mats**—You'll need Bibles, white construction paper, and markers. Form pairs and assign each pair one of the following scripture passages: John 6:26-35; 6:47-58; 8:21-24; 10:1-18; 12:20-26; 13:5-17; 13:33-35; 14:1-6; 14:12-14; 15:1-8; 15:12-17; and 15:18-21.

Distribute paper and markers. Have pairs work together to make place mats for breakfast by writing their scripture on their construction paper and drawing a face that illustrates how the truth in the scripture makes them feel.

Friendship Walk #1—You'll need a Bible, sheet of paper, and pencil for every two people. Give each pair a Bible, a sheet of paper, and pencil. Have pairs write down these tasks to complete while going for a walk together before breakfast.

Find two things that illustrate God's truth.

Find two things that illustrate the world's lies.

Talk about one time a truth helped you and a lie hurt you.

Pray for God to reveal his truths to each of you.

True Calisthenics—You'll need a cassette player and some fast, upbeat, Christian music. Recruit an exercise leader and have kids do aerobics or calisthenics together to Christian music.

Captured Sheep Bible Study—For each person you'll need an 8×10 sheet of posterboard, 30-inch length of string, a Bible, a marker, scissors, and 5-foot length of rope. Say: **Lots of people want us to believe what they say is the truth. But who can you believe?**

Give kids each an 8×10 sheet of posterboard, a 30-inch length of string, a Bible, and a marker. Have kids each take a turn punching a hole on either side of their posterboard with scissors. Then have them each tie the ends of their string to the holes.

Form three groups. Assign each participant in the first group one of the "Worldly Lies" words. Ask kids to each look up and read John 15:1-11 and Galatians 5:22-23, and then write their "worldly lie" on their posterboard. Then give them each a 5-foot length of rope and ask them to tie one end to their wrist.

Assign the second group of kids each one of the "Godly Truths" words. Ask those kids to look up and read John 15:1-11 and Galatians 5:17-21, and then write their "godly truth" on their posterboard. Give them each a 5-foot length of rope and ask them to tie one end to their wrist.

Worldly Lies	Godly Truths
Pornography	● Love
Sexual Freedom	● Joy
Fame	● Peace
Satanism	● Patience
Violence	● Kindness
Back-Stabbing	● Goodness
Look out for #1	● Faithfulness
Have It Your Way	● Gentleness
Rebellion	● Self-Control
Cliques	● Humility
Get What Others Have	● Be Content With What You Have
Drink Alcohol	● Worship God Alone
Do Drugs	● Service
Party All the Time	● Obedience

Have the last group of kids play the role of sheep in this activity. Have them each read John 10:1-18, then draw the outline of a sheep on their posterboard.

Have kids place their posterboard signs around their necks.

Then say: **The people who have worldly lies or godly truths around their necks should try to tag as many sheep as they can. When you tag a sheep, that person must tie part of your rope onto his or her wrist. Then, together, try to tag more sheep. The person who tags and ties the most people wins.**

When all the sheep have been tagged, have each roped-together team (a team can be one person) sit down. Give each team a Bible and a marker.

Say: **All of us are sheep. We're pursued by the truth of God and by the lies of Satan. For those in a worldly lie team, write on your posterboard signs reasons your lie "captures" people. For example, you could write that cliques capture people because they give them a sense of belonging. For those in a godly truth team, write on your posterboard signs reasons it's better to be captured by your specific truth than by any of the lies the world offers. For example, you could write that self-control can keep you from making disastrous choices.**

After 10 minutes, have tied-together teams each come to the

front and explain what they've written on their posterboard signs.

Ask: **Why does Jesus compare people to sheep? What are some ways to avoid being captured by worldly lies? What are some ways to be captured by God's truth? How does it feel to know that Jesus laid down his life for you? How can you lay down your life for Jesus?**

Have kids read aloud Psalm 23 in unison.

● **VISA Card Blues**—You'll need a loaf of bread, a VISA card, and a Bible. For each person you'll need a sheet of construction paper and a marker. Sit in a circle around the construction paper and markers. Ask kids each to make a large VISA card on their construction paper. Show your VISA card as an example. On the back of the card have kids each list all the things they'd charge if they had a $5,000 credit limit.

Ask kids each to tell about their list of charged items.

Ask: **Aren't charge cards great? With them, we can buy almost anything we want at any time. But what's the hidden trap in charging something on a VISA card? Does credit distort the truth? Why or why not? How might drinking, having sex, doing cocaine, speeding, or cheating on tests be like using a VISA card?**

Set out the bread and read aloud John 6:35.

Ask: **If Jesus is the "bread of life," what's the "bread of death"? When was the last time you were hungry or thirsty for something you couldn't have right away? How is Jesus the bread of life to us? If you follow Jesus, are you less tempted to eat the bread of death? Why or why not?**

Give each person a piece of bread to eat.

● **Friendship Walk #2**—You'll need Bibles, paper, and pencils. Form new pairs and give each pair a Bible, a sheet of paper, and pencil. Have kids repeat the tasks from "Friendship Walk #1."

● **"They Want Me to What?" Skit Planning**—You'll need an array of props that could be used to produce a TV commercial such as construction paper, markers, tape, newsprint, clothing, brushes, combs, toothbrushes, or soap. Form teams of three.

Say: **Tonight we'll see just how well you can sell something that's totally useless to a gullible audience. Each team's task is to create and present a TV commercial for a product or** service that really doesn't do what you say it does. For example, you could create a commercial for a mouthwash that actually dissolves teeth. Your goal is to entice the audience to buy the product or service, anyway. We'll videotape the skits and watch them at the end of the evening.

Show groups the props available and offer creative help when needed. Gives teams a few minutes to create their skits.

● **"They Want Me to What?" Skits**—You'll need a video camera and a blank tape.

Recruit an enthusiastic announcer to introduce the skits and someone to videotape each one. Decide on an order for the skits, and then set kids loose.

After the groups finish performing, ask: **Why is advertising sometimes so deceiving? When have you been burned by an advertising claim? How do you know if you're listening to a truth or a lie?**

● **Journey of Light**—You'll need the "Journey-of-Light Cards" on page 145 photocopied and cut apart, and eight candles, eight matchbooks, and a flashlight. Ask for eight volunteer readers. Give each one a candle and a matchbook.

Take your group on a night walk. During the walk, stop four times and sit in the darkness for a while. At each stop have two volunteer readers light their candles and read aloud the corresponding "Lucifer" and "Jesus" cards. Then ask kids to discuss what's appealing about both claims and how to choose between the two. Have an adult leader carry the flashlight.

● **Not-Ready-for-Prime-Time Video Event**—You'll need the videotape of the "They Want Me to What?" skits, a VCR and monitor, popcorn, and soft drinks. Set up the VCR and monitor, and then play the videotape of the "They Want Me to What?" skits. Serve refreshments while kids watch their skits on video.

● **Light of the World Evensong**—You'll need candles, matches and a Bible. Give each person a candle. Sit in a circle and turn out the lights. Light your candle and read aloud John 8:12. Then light your neighbor's candle and finish the statement, "If I let Jesus be my light, I can bring light to someone else by..." Have kids each finish the statement as they light their neighbor's candle. Close by singing a favorite worship chorus.

JOURNEY-OF-LIGHT CARDS

Lucifer Card #1
I am Lucifer, Prince of Darkness.
Come, follow me, and I will teach you to hate.

Jesus Card #1
I am Jesus, Prince of Light.
Come, follow me, and I will teach you to love one another.

Lucifer Card #2
I am Lucifer, Prince of Darkness. Come, follow me, and you can have all
the physical pleasures of your wildest dreams.

Jesus Card #2
I am Jesus, Prince of Light.
Worship the Lord your God and serve him only.

Lucifer Card #3
I am Lucifer, Prince of Darkness. Come follow me
and I will teach you to cheat, lie, and steal.

Jesus Card #3
I am Jesus, Prince of Light. Come, follow me,
and I will show you the way, the truth, and the life.

Lucifer Card #4
I am Lucifer, Prince of Darkness. Come, follow me,
and I will teach you how to conquer others.

Jesus Card #4
I am Jesus, Prince of Light. Come, follow me,
and you will learn forgiveness and grace.

● **Friendship Walk #3**—Form new pairs and give each pair a Bible, a sheet of paper, and pencil. Have kids repeat the tasks from "Friendship Walks #1 and #2."

● **True Calisthenics**—You'll need a cassette player and some fast, upbeat Christian music. Recruit an exercise leader and have kids do aerobics or calisthenics together to Christian music.

● **True Worship Preparation**—You'll need Bibles, songbooks, newsprint, markers, pencils, construction paper, and scissors. Form five groups. Assign each group one of the following tasks:

Group 1—Design an opening activity that'll help people focus on worshiping God.

Group 2—Design a creative process for participants to confess their sins.

Group 3—Choose songs, and then lead the group in singing and giving thanks to God.

Group 4—Make a gift that each person will receive during worship.

Group 5—Creatively present the "Jesus Card" statements from the "Journey-of-Light Cards."

True Worship—Have kids present the worship service combining the five elements. As a closing activity, have kids discover who their "Lie Buster" has been.

RETREAT OUTLINE #2

Thanksgiving as a Way of Life

"Everybody at lunch was talking about how bad their life is—how much arguing there is at home and how bad their parents treat them. I thought to myself that I have life easy," my daughter told me one day. Then she continued, "You know, I forgot all about having cancer."

That's the essence of thankfulness—a view of life that notices more good than bad, a view that finds joy regardless of the circumstances. This retreat guides you to cultivate that kind of thankfulness in your kids.

OBJECTIVES

During this retreat participants will
- identify the need for a thankful life,
- practice thankfulness,
- examine thankfulness myths, and
- commit to a thankful lifestyle.

RETREAT PREPARATION

● **Overcomer or Overcome?**—Ask two volunteers to prepare five-minute monologues about what their life has been like, the relationships they've had, and what they've believed about whether God treated them fairly. Both characters are in their 80s and have never married. One has lived an empty life of bitterness, and the other has lived a fruitful life of thanksgiving.

● **Devotion Commotion**—Write each of the following instructions on separate sheets of newsprint.

"**Call to Worship**—Search Psalm 103 for verses to read at the start of worship."

"**Music**—Choose songs or choruses to thank God."

"**Prayer**—Compose prayer starters or a litany of praise."

"**Message**—Choose one of the passages from this weekend and prepare to talk about it."

"**Commitment**—Prepare an opportunity for kids to commit to a thankful lifestyle."

RETREAT SCHEDULE

Friday

8 p.m.	Group Names
8:45 p.m.	Grouch-Grabbers
9:15 p.m.	Grumbles
10 p.m.	Gratitude Chains

Saturday

8 a.m.	Breakfast
9 a.m.	Ovations
9:45 a.m.	Ouch!
10:30 a.m.	Optimism Practiced
11:45 a.m.	Optical Adjustment

12:30 p.m. Lunch
1:15 p.m. Thanksgiving Scavenger Hunt
2 p.m.   Free Time
4 p.m.   Organized Games
5:30 p.m. Supper
6:30 p.m. Overcomer or Overcome?
7:15 p.m. Odious Thanksgiving
8 p.m.   Snack Break
10 p.m.   Opinions

Sunday
8 a.m.   Breakfast
9:15 a.m. Devotion Commotion
10 a.m.   Declare Thanks
11:30 a.m. Depart

THE RETREAT

Friday

● **Grump Snacks**—You'll need horseradish, crackers, and sweet candies. Spread horseradish on crackers. As kids leave for the retreat site, pop a cracker with horseradish in each mouth. Explain that complaining tastes bad and makes life hard to swallow. Let kids carry the bitter taste throughout the trip. When they arrive, pop a sweet candy in each person's mouth.

Say: **You've had a bitter taste in your mouth. The candy takes away that bitter taste. In the same way, thankfulness can take away the bitterness of a bad experience.**

● **Group Names**—You'll need paper and pencils. Form groups of four. Have each group draw a circle on a sheet of paper. Have group members each name one thing they're thankful for. If the others in the group agree about that thing, have that person write it in the circle. If there isn't unanimous agreement, write the item outside the circle. Continue until there are eight items in the circle. Using those words, have each group choose a name. For example, if a group is thankful for sunshine and candy, it might choose "Sweet Sunshine" as a name. Have groups report their names.

● **Grouch-Grabbers**—You'll need balloons, markers, and sandwich bags. Have kids each blow up and tie off a balloon, write a

147

problem on it, and use a 3-foot string to attach the balloon to one ankle. Challenge kids to pop other balloons while protecting their own. After the game, ask: **How did you feel during this activity? How did you try to protect your balloon? How do people try to hang on to problems?**

Have kids gather up the burst balloon pieces and place them all in one sandwich bag. Say: **We can still see our problems and worries, but they don't have to control us. Let's discover ways to handle problems instead of allowing them to handle us.**

● **Grumbles**—You'll need balloons, markers, and tape. Distribute more balloons to each named group. Have them blow up and tie off the balloons, write one thing to grumble about on each balloon, then tape their balloons to a wall designated for that group. Challenge each group to create the fullest "grumble wall."

Have kids line up in two lines facing each other. Identify one line as grumblers and one line as thankers. Name a situation. Call for grumblers to tell rotten things about it and the thankers to tell good things. Use situations such as "no date on Friday night," "windy day," "diagnosed with a serious disease," "failed a test," "got cut from a team," "hair flopped," and "nuclear war."

Ask: **How do you feel when you grumble? when you're thankful? What happens when you grumble? give thanks?**

● **Gratitude Chains**—You'll need tape and a stack of 3×5 cards. Throughout the weekend, encourage named groups to write on each card one thing they're thankful for and tape their cards end to end. Have groups compete to make the longest chain.

Saturday

● **Ovations**—You'll need paper and pencils. Have kids each tell something they're thankful for, then pop a balloon on their wall. Continue until all the balloons are popped. Lead kids in singing songs of thanksgiving such as "Thank You, Lord."

Read aloud 1 Thessalonians 5:16-18.

Ask: **What is God's will for us? What two actions often precede giving thanks in all circumstances?**

Describe "joy" not only as a feeling, but also as confidence based on the assurance that God cares.

● **Ouch!**—You'll need dominoes. Form two teams. Have teams race to build 10-story houses out of dominoes. Houses will probably keep falling. After 10 minutes, ask: **How did you feel during this activity? What can you be thankful about in this situation? What similar discouraging experiences have you had? Did you respond with thankfulness or complaining?**

● **Optimism Practiced**—Say: **Thankfulness is action and attitude as well as words. Rather than grumbling "not fair," act to find ways through problems.**

Read aloud 1 Peter 4:12-19. Ask: **Which actions show thankfulness? which attitudes? Which of these is easiest? hardest?**

● **Optical Adjustment**—You'll need pipe cleaners.

Say: **Six blind men encounter an elephant and study it to discover what it's like. The first feels its side and declares the elephant is like a wall. The second strokes its tusk and says it's more like a spear. The third takes the trunk and determines it's like a snake. The fourth feels its knee and concludes it's like a tree. The fifth touches the ear and says an elephant is like a fan. The sixth feels its tail and says it's like a rope. Each man defends his opinion strongly and stiffly. Though each is partly right, they all are wrong.**

Ask: **How does perspective affect how you feel about life? How is God's perspective different from yours?**

Explain to kids that God has the power to get them through pain, and he offers good even in the midst of a bad situation. Have kids tell about a time God brought good out of pain.

Give kids pipe cleaners. Have them make glasses and wear them as a commitment to see life from God's perspective.

● **Thanksgiving Scavenger Hunt**—You'll need a chocolate bar. Form pairs. Have pairs work together to find an item they can thank God for that begins with each letter of the word "thanksgiving." For example, kids could bring back a **t**histle and say it reminds them to thank God even when bad things happen, a **h**at because it helps them look cool, an **a**pple because it tastes good, and so on. The first pair to return with all the items wins a giant chocolate bar (because everyone's thankful for chocolate!).

● **Overcomer or Overcome?**—Introduce your two "elderly" characters. Explain that each person experienced the same situation in life—never marrying. Each responded differently to the circumstance. Have each dramatist present his or her monologue.

Ask: **What are the results of a bitter life? a thankful life? Why are thankful people happy people?**

● **Odious Thanksgiving**—Read aloud Luke 18:9-14.

Ask: **What's wrong with the Pharisee's thankfulness?**

Form pairs. Give pairs three minutes to discuss what's wrong with each of these statements, "You should thank God for giving you cancer," "I can't be sad, because I'm a Christian," and "I feel better when I compare my problems to yours."

Ask: **How do these statements reduce compassion? What other bad examples of thankfulness have you seen?**

● **Opinions**—Designate separate walls as "agree," "disagree," "strongly agree," or "strongly disagree." Tell kids to stand by the wall that tells how they feel about each of the following statements:

1. Being thankful when bad things happen means you're ignoring your problems.

2. You can't be thankful and angry at the same time.

3. If we're truly grateful, we won't grieve or be sad.

4. Thankfulness is being grateful God is with me.

Say: **Thankfulness can occur with any emotion. In fact, it's important to be honest about how you feel. Giving thanks in all things doesn't mean to thank God for problems but to thank God for his presence as you go through them.**

Sunday

● **Devotion Commotion**—Tape the instructions you prepared beforehand around the room. Have kids go to any of the five worship stations and prepare for worship.

● **Declare Thanks**—You'll need fruit. Call on each group to lead its portion of worship. Declare a winner in the "Gratitude Chain" contest. Reward the winners with fruit, because a thankful life yields good fruit.

Conclude the worship by saying: **We don't have to depend on circumstances for happiness. God gives us something to be thankful for in every circumstances.**

Close in prayer, asking God to help kids live thankful lives.

MORE RESOURCES FOR A DYNAMIC YOUTH MINISTRY

The 13 Most Important Bible Lessons for Teenagers

Build a strong foundation of basic Bible understanding with these active lessons that make learning fun. You'll get 13 complete programs on topics like...

- Who is Jesus?
- What is the Bible?
- Why does life hurt?
- Why the church?

...plus, you'll teach lessons on prayer, witnessing, practical service, and end times. Perfect to help new Christians understand their faith or to refresh mature believers. The 13-week format works well for Sunday school or youth meetings.

ISBN 1-55945-261-7

Building Community in Youth Groups

Denny Rydberg

Transform your group into a warm, caring community. You'll learn a practical five-step process of...

- Bond Building—establishing trust in your group,
- Opening Up—creating a freedom to talk and listen,
- Affirmation—offering sincere compliments to others,
- Stretching—experiencing challenging growth, and
- Goal Setting—becoming more accountable to one another.

Each step is supported with loads of ready-to-use, creative activities and discussion ideas. Plus, you'll find detailed, step-by-step meeting and retreat plans.

ISBN 0-931529-06-9

Creative Worship Ideas

This new worship resource book is packed with creative ideas to get young people involved in leading worship. Instead of dozing through the service or not coming to church at all, teenagers will discover the joy of worship as they actively participate. And pastors will appreciate the wealth of unique program ideas to keep the worship experience fresh and inviting for their congregations. This practical worship-planning tool includes...

- •creative prayers,
- •unique Scripture readings and studies,
- •fresh ideas for music and singing,
- •fun skits that point to biblical truths,
- •unforgettable, teen-generated messages,

...plus, complete services for special occasions such as commissioning groups for service projects, and celebrating Christian holidays with pizazz. Not just for Sunday morning, these ideas can spice up any worship experience whether in the sanctuary, home, or by the campfire.

ISBN 1-55945-099-1

Do It! Active Learning in Youth Ministry

Thom and Joani Schultz

Discover the keys to teaching creative faith-building lessons that teenagers look forward to...and remember for a lifetime. You'll learn how to design simple, fun programs that will help your kids...

- •build community,
- •develop communication skills,
- •relate better to others,
- •experience what it's really like to be a Christian,

...and apply the Bible to their daily challenges. Plus, you'll get 24 ready-to-use active-learning exercises complete with debriefing questions and Bible application. For example, your kids will...

- •learn the importance of teamwork and the value of each team member by juggling six different objects as a group,
- •experience community and God's grace using a doughnut,
- •grow more sensitive to others' needs by acting out Matthew 25:31-46

...just to name a few. And the practical index of over 30 active-learning resources will make your planning easier.

ISBN 0-931529-94-8

Order today from your local Christian bookstore, or write: Group Publishing, Box 485, Loveland, CO 80539. For mail orders, please add postage/handling of $4 for orders up to $15, $5 for orders of $15.01+. Colorado residents add 3% sales tax.

GET YOUR KIDS TALKING AND LOOKING TO THE BIBLE...

Get your kids and adults really talking with this exciting new video series complete with leaders guide. Each hot topic is guaranteed to start discussions and motivate your viewers to explore Scripture for answers to their tough, thought-provoking questions. All segments are real—not staged or acted out.

The video format makes for easy use. Preview the appropriate video and Leaders Guide section before using with your group. Then, follow the suggested format to get the most out of each segment with your group...

- open the meeting with one of the openers listed;
- work through the exercises included;
- play the segment of the tape to your group;
- use the Leaders Guide to encourage the conversations that develop; and
- close by choosing one of the closing options listed.

The leaders guide also helps prepare you to deal with the conversations that develop. Information for each video segment includes...

- meeting plans for each topic,
- appropriate Scripture to guide biblical conversations,
- lesson objectives,
- photocopiable handouts to get your group involved in the lesson, and
- statistics and other tips that support the segment topic.

Don't waste another meeting in silence. Start your group talking with **Group's Hot Talk-Starter Videos**.

SERIES 1

Teen Suicide•An Atheist's Beliefs•Dating: He Says/She Says•Teenagers in the KKK   ISBN 1-55945-259-5

SERIES 2

Pregnant Teenager•R-Rated Movies•What's a Monk?•Hooked on Gambling

ISBN 1-55945-274-9

SERIES 3

The Rapture of 1992 (Part 1)•The Rapture of 1992 (Part 2)•Underage Smoker•A Visit to a New Age Store•The Gang Life   ICDN 1 66016 076 7

SERIES 4

Gay Rights•Palm Reading•Body Image: Glamour Shots•Homeless Teenagers

ISBN 1-55945-276-5

Hot Talk-Starter Set (all four series)   ISBN 1-55945-277-3

WARNING: These video programs deal with sensitive issues and do not supply conclusions. Preview segments before use. Prepare your discussion leaders using the accompanying guide. Use these presentations only when accompanied by a careful debriefing time.

Order today from your local Christian bookstore, or write: Group Publishing, Box 485, Loveland, CO 80539. For mail orders, please add postage/handling of $4 for orders up to $15, $5 for orders of $15.01+. Colorado residents add 3% sales tax.